Tragedies of Our Own Making

How Private Choices Have
Created Public Bankruptcy

Tragedies of Our Own Making

Richard Neely

University of Illinois Press Urbana and Chicago

This book is printed on acid-free paper.

Library of Congress Cataloging-in-Publication Data

Neely, Richard, 1941–
    Tragedies of our own making : how private choices have created
public bankruptcy / Richard Neely.
        p.   cm.
    Includes index.
    ISBN 0-252-02038-3
    1. Budget deficits–United States. 2. Debts, Public–United
States. 3. Bankruptcy–United States. 4. United States–Economic
conditions–1981– 5. United States–Social conditions–1980–
I. Title.
HJ2051.N38   1994
336.3'4'0973–dc20   93-43075
                                                                  CIP

For my mother,
Elinore Forlani Neely,
who did everything right

A wise tory and a wise whig, I believe, will agree. Their principles are the same, though their modes of thinking are different.

—Samuel Johnson

Contents

Acknowledgments

Many contributed to this book. My close friend R. Witter Hallan devoted many Saturday nights to explaining why people are skeptical of "family values" and traditional family life. Without him, the tone of this book might have been more hard-hearted. My administrative assistant Debra Atkins typed manuscript drafts and scrutinized the material to ensure its clarity. My law clerk Kathleen Gross helped me to appreciate how professional women feel about the conflict between work and child care and enlightened me to the perspective of young working women. My former law clerk Scott Jones alerted me to the attitudes, opinions, and anxieties of young adults so that this book might speak convincingly to the generation about to begin family life.

Another former law clerk, Douglas Kornreich, is largely responsible for the book's statistical research. Not just a brilliant lawyer, Douglas is also a brilliant statistical analyst and computer programmer. In addition to slaving over budget digests and spending hours on the telephone with the staffs of state legislative finance committees, Douglas made frequent trips to Charlottesville to tap the resources of the University of Virginia library system.

My current law clerk Lisa Reisman arrived, brandishing her classics degrees, in time to do a masterful editing job. She eliminated surplus verbiage and rewrote cumbersome prose. Geoffrey Frank at the "Outlook" section of the *Washington Post* and Grant Ujifusa at *Readers' Digest* helped me separate important new insights into the nature of social insurance systems and the dynamics of state budgets from family-values-type arguments that everyone has heard before.

I am also grateful to my editor Richard Wentworth and to the University of Illinois Press. This is not a "politically correct" book from anyone's point of view. I am too agnostic about morality for the right and too censorious about private conduct for the left. Dick Wentworth encouraged me to write the book, these shortcomings notwithstanding.

Finally, I thank my agent Marian Young for her efforts. Academic books are notoriously unprofitable, yet Marian has always seen to it that my books are published. Without Marian to keep me company through the tribulations of writing about serious social problems, I'd leave government and practice law.

Introduction

State judges have in common with undertakers the fact that eventually everybody drops by to see us. In state court we see budget fights, welfare rights litigation, school battles, every species of delinquency and child neglect, plus a full rogues' gallery of criminals. Twenty years as a judge has convinced me that state government fiscal crises, deteriorating schools, declining living standards among the old blue-collar class, and our rising crime rate are all strangely interrelated.

I am a yellow dog Democrat.[1] In my entire life I have voted for exactly five Republicans—three judges, a close friend, and a fellow running against a Democrat who was worse than a yellow dog. I have no love for policies that favor the rich, yet it was not Republican parsimony toward social programs in the Reagan-Bush years that bankrupted state and local government. Rather, it was our unsuccessful attempt to transfer family responsibilities to government agencies that did us in financially.

Our state and local governments can no longer meet their existing obligations, which means they are bankrupt. Everywhere the budgets for essential government services like education, police protection, health department inspections, criminal courts, and road repair are being pillaged to pay for welfare-related and family substitute programs. By welfare-related and family substitute programs, I do not mean just "welfare checks" (AFDC), but the cost of public housing, battered children's shelters, efforts to collect child support, foster care, programs for latchkey children, residential treatment facilities for law-breaking juveniles, and, steepest of all, medicaid. The collapse of state and local government, however, is only one symptom of a

---

1. A yellow dog Democrat is someone who would vote for a yellow dog if it were on the ballot as a Democratic nominee.

broader economic, educational, and social collapse that no govern-ment-funded social programs can remedy.

By economic collapse, I mean the steady erosion in the living stan-dard of the bottom half of our labor force. The deterioration in real wages for unskilled and semiskilled workers occurring since 1980 results from a convergence of international competition for low-skill work and our own failure to teach basic literacy and numeracy skills to the roughly 50 percent of our children who are disadvantaged in one way or another. Yet it is not because our schools are inferior by world standards that they fail us, but because millions of our children come to school so neglected and distraught over their desperate per-sonal circumstances that they are unable to learn.

Figure 1, prepared by the Centers for Disease Control, presents the point clearly. The child of a never-married mother is three times more likely to be expelled from school than the child of a two-parent fami-ly, and the child of a never-married mother is almost three times more likely than a child of a two-parent family to repeat a grade.[2] Further-more, the same bleak personal circumstances that cause our children to fail in school also engender our rising rate of violent crime, our burgeoning underclass population, and the progressive degeneration of our public places. Indeed, if we control for family configuration, the correlation disappears between race and crime and between low income and crime.[3]

When I was first elected to office in the early seventies, I was deter-mined to make social programs work. As a state legislator, I sponsored bills to expand West Virginia's student loan program, allow the elder-ly to ride school buses free of charge, and create a community mental health system. As judge a few years later, I held the conditions in West Virginia's mental hospitals unconstitutional because of their "Dicken-sian squalor of unconscionable magnitude." I also wrote opinions clos-ing West Virginia's reform schools because of their brutality and re-vamped domestic law to facilitate divorcing mothers getting custody of their children without trading away needed support money.[4] Dur-

2. See U. S. Dept. of Health and Human Services, Public Health Service, Centers for Disease Control, National Center for Health Statistics, Hyattsville, Md., June 1991, DHHS Publication Number (PHS) 91–1506.
3. See W. Grove and R. Crutchfield, "The Family and Juvenile Delinquency," *Socio-logical Quarterly* (Summer 1982); for additional examples, see the sources cited in chapters 5 and 6.

Figure 1. Percent of Children 5–17 Who Had Ever Experienced
Selected Academic Problems, by Family Type (United States, 1988)

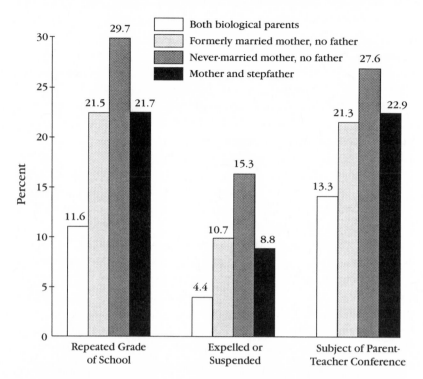

Source: Nicholas Zill and Charlotte Schoenborn, "Developmental Learning and Emotional
Problems: Health of Our Nation's Children, U.S. 1988," *Advanced Data from Vital and Health
Statistics* (Hyattsville: National Center for Health Statistics, 1990), 190.

ing the late 1970s I spent so much time with West Virginia's commissioner of human services, Leon Ginsberg, out on the street at night
trying to make the social services delivery system work that the
Charleston Daily Mail dubbed the two of us "Batman and Robin."

Ultimately, all of us who believed that government might provide
workable family substitutes failed because the demands to transfer
family costs to government programs far outstripped government's
ability to pay. When a fourteen-year-old girl has a premature baby, it

4. For details of this, see Richard Neely, "The Primary Caretaker Parent Rule: Child
Custody and the Dynamics of Greed," *Yale Law and Policy Review* 3 (1985): 168.

costs medicaid $2,000 a day for about a hundred days. Despite statistics that show adolescent girls having premature babies at about four times the rate for mature women, the number of pregnant, unmarried teenagers increases every year. The costs of this increase defy comprehension: Four cases of premature birth will eat the entire Public Radio budget for a medium-size state!

If we find a hundred children who desperately need a staff-secure residential school with competent psychiatric treatment, by the time we get the facility built and staffed we need an additional hundred beds. And this, perhaps, is why I am letting the greedy Republicans of the Reagan-Bush years off the hook so easily: New programs funded by progressive taxes between 1980 and 1993 would have done *nothing* but postpone for two or three years the inevitable public bankruptcy that we now see all around us. Until we stabilize the size of the population in need of government services, we cannot reverse America's steep educational, economic, and social decline.

This book is not about nostalgia, for nostalgia will do little to stave off our public bankruptcy. Millions of Americans yearn for yesteryear, when the natural order of things was self-evident. Father worked, mother stayed home with the children, divorce was sanctioned, sex was unmentionable, a teen-age girl who became pregnant hid from society, homosexuals were sent to prison, literature and movies were censored, and drugs were unknown. That world is gone forever, not because pointy-headed, left-wing, granola-eating, atheist intellectuals have captured control of the government, but because most blue-collar and middle-class, church-going, hard-working Americans *want* that world to be gone forever.

In social issues Americans overwhelmingly support a live-and-let-live approach to the private matters of sex and family. Referenda at the state level circumscribing the rights of gays and lesbians fail as often as they pass, and those narrowing welfare rights generally fail. Legislatures regularly loosen the divorce laws, and judges consistently side with "modern values" against "traditional values" on questions of sexuality, abortion, and lifestyle. These are all democratic decisions, and they demonstrate conclusively that we are not going to return to the moralizing social paradigm of 1950. A new value system in sharp distinction to that of today will necessarily emerge from the government bankruptcy and social collapse that I forecast in this book, but that new value system will not be a replay of yesteryear.

None of this, of course, makes any sense until we begin to examine the hard numbers of public bankruptcy and the overwhelming evidence of educational, economic, and social collapse. In fiscal year 1992-93, California had more than a $14 billion budget gap, the budget gap of the state of New York exceeded $6 billion, and most other state governments—including Illinois, Pennsylvania, Massachusetts, and Maryland—experienced serious financial problems. What's draining these state budgets are welfare, medicaid, and programs that provide direct services to families and children.

Economists understand that good macroeconomics (i.e., the management of the whole economy) depend upon good microeconomics (i.e., the management of individual firms). Third world countries quickly discovered after independence that no amount of government tinkering could substitute for innovative managers, skilled labor forces, and sound infrastructure like railroads, telephones, and electricity. Likewise, the success of the *public* safety net in any country depends on the success of the *private* safety net, and the private safety net is the family. Blaming our rising crime rate, our increasingly uncompetitive labor force, and our rising number of poor children on "inadequate" social programs is simple denial. We currently spend more money per capita in real, inflation-adjusted dollars on all social programs put together than at any other time in America's history, yet every year the pathologies that social programs are designed to heal become more irremediable.

Illegitimacy, divorce, and parental neglect are bankrupting us. The most incurable pathologies, or course, are found among the underclass in the inner cities, but overall our problems emanate far more from middle-class whites than poor blacks. It is, after all, the white middle class who still set the tone for everyone else, and among the white middle class illegitimacy, divorce, and parental neglect are rampant. In Clay County, West Virginia, the black population is one-tenth of one percent, while the illegitimacy rate is 29.5 percent. *White* illegitimacy alone in the United States today exceeds 19 percent. For every one illegitimate black birth, there are 1.3 illegitimate white births.[5]

5. In 1989, there were 593,900 illegitimate white births in the United States and 457,500 illegitimate black births. In 1970, however, there were many more black illegitimate births than white illegitimate births: 215,100 to 175,100, or 1.23 black illegitimate births for every white illegitimate birth. In a mere twenty years, the situation had

We have always had illegitimacy, divorce, and severely stressed parents. Thirty years ago when we weren't going bankrupt, and living standards were doubling every generation, however, society was dominated by stable, two-parent families where one parent stayed home to care for children. Therefore, it is not illegitimacy, divorce, and parental labor force participation per se that are killing us, but rather the rate at which these phenomena relentlessly increase year after year. More than half of mothers with preschool children worked outside the home in 1991, compared with one in five in 1960. About 27 percent of all U.S. infants today are born to unmarried women and girls—up from 18.4 percent in 1980, 10.7 percent in 1970, and 5.3 percent in 1960. As I shall explain in this book, however, there is something we can do about all this that doesn't cost very much money.

All social programs—whether the benefits are paid in cash or in kind—are based on insurance principles. This basic truth is often obscured by today's fashion of calling government benefits "entitlements." Yet the insurance nature of social programs should be obvious upon a moment's reflection: We all pay part of our taxes into a pot so that when one of us suffers a tragedy, like becoming a widow or giving birth to a retarded child, we can draw on that pot to get us past the hard times. When we set up welfare, unemployment compensation, and other types of social insurance in the Roosevelt administration, we assumed that people would act responsibly and attempt to limit losses.

Today, voluntary decisions are increasing the loss rate to such a point that our safety net mechanisms can no longer be viewed in any reasonable sense as "insurance." We have, in effect, converted a comparatively cheap yet highly comprehensive social insurance system into an exorbitant, overtaxed, and largely incompetent general subsidy program. Moreover, because of the dynamics of all bureaucracies, any transfer of private, family-related costs to public budgets always occurs at a huge net cost increase. It is our social insurance premiums, then, that act both to raise taxes and to devour the other state and local programs that I mentioned earlier. In West Virginia, the state medicaid budget now equals the state budget for education at all levels, and this is typical of almost all other states.

---

turned exactly around, and the gap continues to grow. See Table 87, *Statistical Abstract of the United States* (1992).

When the "loss rate" in any insurance program increases substantially, either premiums must go up or coverage must go down; both of these undesirable results can be observed in every American social program today. In constant 1983 dollars, welfare payments currently amount to only about 75 percent of what they were a decade ago, while medicaid reimbursements are now so low that doctors are abandoning inner-city and rural practices in unprecedented numbers. Taxes everywhere are going up while quality is going down in the provision of all social services—everything from public housing to public hospitals.

Real insurance can protect against only accidental losses. That is why fire insurance works year in and year out without significant increases in premiums while social insurance doesn't. In fire insurance, homeowners take extraordinary precautions to keep their houses from burning down, which means a constant loss rate. But, if homeowners decided that the easy way to change neighborhoods or refurbish their interiors was to be negligent about turning off the stove, fire insurance premiums would go through the roof, and the fire insurance industry would go bankrupt.

In our social insurance system we are going broke because we are allowing excessive losses to be triggered through carelessness. Millions of children will be born to parents who will needlessly divorce, making those children uncared for and insecure. Illegitimacy and divorce are to social insurance what leaving a pot of oil on a burning stove is to fire insurance. Obviously, as soon as losses become rampant through carelessness, we no longer have an insurance program but, rather, something else. Increasingly that "something else" is not politically acceptable, which is why the middle class won't pay taxes.

Ironically, welfare and its related medicaid costs are not state government's biggest problem. We could probably keep the current welfare system pretty much intact were it not that the same behavior that raises our welfare bill also causes crime, school failure, and labor force deterioration. Anyone who has raised children and monitored their school progress understands that it is the rare child who does well in school without a lot of parental coaching. Children don't do their homework without someone standing over them: I never did, and I am willing to bet that the reader never did. Public schools are far from perfect, but they are much better than they are ever given credit for, and they are also probably better funded and better staffed than the schools of any other country. The truth, then, is that our public schools (except, perhaps, in ritzy, upper-middle-class suburbs) are failing because teachers can't teach when there is no back-up at home.

All public agencies—welfare departments, domestic courts, and the public health departments—are crumbling under the burden of acting as a surrogate family. When middle-class taxpayers dig in their heels over taxes, as they did throughout the Reagan-Bush years, demand for social services skyrockets while appropriations remain stagnant. Use of overburdened domestic courts, health department clinics, and public legal services is rationed by unconscionably long waits, while child foster care, drug and alcohol treatment, and shelters for the homeless are rationed by steady service deterioration. In this last regard, Democrats must stop denying the evidence before their own eyes: The real world of deteriorating public services stands in stark contrast to the prevailing political claptrap about new social programs. Old-style tax-tax, spend-spend liberalism in the 1990s is right out of *Alice's Adventures in Wonderland*. We can still have humane and caring government, but the techniques must change significantly from yesteryear if we are to sustain the support of the middle class.

My work on neighborhood crime control has revealed again and again the absence of any adult presence during the weekday hours when children are home from school in most working-class, middle-class, and, in many places, even upper-middle-class neighborhoods. West Virginia has America's lowest crime rate because West Virginia has by far America's lowest female labor force participation rate.[6] West Virginia also has a higher than normal incidence of close, extended families. The simple correlation between low crime and stay-at-home parents so strikingly evident in West Virginia demonstrates that we can't continue to ignore our children the way we have since the seventies without inviting more of the crime and savagery we have watched grow for the past twenty years.

Unfortunately, trying to influence voluntary behavior in a positive way invites charges of "racism," "sexism," and "elitism" from nincom-

---

6. In 1991, West Virginia's female labor force participation rate was 44.2 percent. The overall female labor force participation rate in the United States is 57.3 percent. No other state has a female labor force participation rate within eight percentage points of West Virginia's. Only eight states have a female labor force participation rate within ten percentage points of West Virginia's. See Table 613, *Statistical Abstract of the United States* (1992).

poops who think they've claimed the politically correct moral high ground. Yet "isms" have nothing to do with the grim numbers concerning government bankruptcy that leap off the page, and "isms" don't alter the fact that the menu of workable solutions to our problems is extraordinarily limited and every choice involves a modification of private behavior. Today's technologies, like the new surgically inserted Norplant birth control device, demonstrate that children are not a natural consequence of sexual freedom.

America's current tolerant attitude toward its underclass and its current commitment to social services are not necessarily set in stone. The last forty years have seen dramatic paradigm shifts throughout American society. All our traditional institutions—the law, religion, and even the state—have changed in startling ways almost overnight. The catalog of paradigm shifts includes the pill, soaring divorce rates, custody battles, poor single-parent households headed by women, right-to-life and pro-choice struggles, two-career families, surrogacy, women's rights, gay rights, battered wives and murdered families, the disappearance of traditional patterns of sexual differentiation, in vitro fertilization, casual attitudes toward sex, and the emergence of an unparalleled level of violence among young American men.

These paradigm shifts demonstrate that America is a volatile society far from immune to dangerous inclinations (as anyone who recalls communism and fascism waiting in the wings for the Roosevelt administration to fail in the late 1930s fully understands). Tolerance of groups who are threatening and destructive is already receding; capital punishment is becoming more prevalent and the criminal law increasingly conservative. Federal courts today have all but abandoned review of state court criminal convictions, and the Supreme Court of the United States has lost interest in the race discrimination issues that naturally arise from any careful analysis of capital punishment. Particularly in the federal courts, where enormous power has been given to life-tenured, civil service prosecutors to terrify defendants through the draconian federal sentencing guidelines into pleading guilty even if they're innocent, criminal law is perceived as nothing more than an adjunct to the waste management industry.

We currently incarcerate a higher percentage of our population than any other developed country, yet prison construction and criminal sanctions cannot be kept ahead of demand. As more and more of suburban and rural America becomes dangerous and unlivable because of new crime threats, cheap, efficient, open-air concentration camps for the underclass in places like Idaho and Montana may begin to look attractive to middle- and working-class taxpayers, along with even more resort to capital punishment. Critics of this book who are tempted to accuse me of "racism," "sexism," or "elitism" must therefore understand that just sitting back and allowing things to continue to run amok while political junkies bicker over how to spend money we don't have on programs that don't work is extraordinarily dangerous.

The purpose of this book is to pull the various strands of our public bankruptcy together so that the entire problem can be viewed at once. The argument that I make here naturally breaks down into six parts, which correspond to the six chapters. In the first chapter I explain to readers who don't work with government budgets all the time the rudiments of government finance and how we pay for social programs. Here I must set out such tedious but crucial things as the natural limits to progressive taxation at the state and local levels. This first chapter is necessary because an extraordinary number of informed and concerned people believe that the solution to our problems is more family substitute programs. Right at the outset I must explain why it is not possible to have free universal day care; why it is not possible to provide adequate support to divorced and never-married single mothers; and why it is not possible to provide good facilities for every disturbed, aggressive, acting-out juvenile.

The second chapter explains how social programs are deteriorating in spite of constant infusions of new money. I explain why public institutions are too corrupt and too incompetent to perform effectively the family responsibilities that we have tried to transfer to them, even when we are willing to pay handsomely. In a nutshell, government is driven by providers and not by consumers, which means that corruption and incompetence will ultimately suck most of the life's blood out of any social program that gives clients in-kind services rather than cash.

Most users of social services are from disorganized constituencies with little political power. The weaker any constituency is politically, the greater the likelihood that the benefits that constituency receives will be in kind rather than in cash. That's because when consumers of government services are weak, they are out-gunned politically by well-organized and well-financed provider interests. The first two chapters consequently explain the ins and outs of government insolvency and social program deterioration and why whenever a private family cost is transferred to the government, the transfer will inevitably occur at an enormous net cost increase.

In the third chapter I begin to explain our metaphorical bankruptcies, turning first to the collapse of public education. What we need far more than better schools is better parents, and I prove my point by comparing American schools to other nations' schools. America has the finest school system in the world, and in the top half of our labor force this fact is conspicuous. However, our schools are not as successful as poorer German, Japanese, and Korean schools in preparing the bottom half of the labor force because disadvantaged children get little help with their homework and come to school burdened by crushing personal problems related primarily to disrupted families.

The fourth chapter deals with falling real wages among the bottom half of the American labor force. Here I explain how educational failure related to family problems, combined with foreign competition for unskilled and semiskilled work, constantly erode the standard of living of the old blue-collar class. The fifth chapter explores the dire social consequences of all this in terms of crime and the crime-related destruction of important public spaces—everything from urban shopping streets to public parks to the campus of Yale University.

In the last chapter I provide a blueprint for solving our problems. America got into its current dilemma over thirty years, and it will take at least half that long to get out. What I propose are cheap and efficient ways to reduce illegitimacy among all groups without compulsion through a massive paid television advertising campaign setting forth objective public health information concerning the dire consequences of illegitimacy and divorce with coordinated television entertainment programs (like the afternoon soap operas used in developing countries to encourage contraception). These techniques will raise society's level of consciousness about what is bankrupting us and change the stories we tell one another about personal responsibility, family, and child care.

Although the measures I propose are revolutionary, they are both cheap and humane. These proposals, I believe, are the type of real change (rather than building bigger models of systems that don't work) that the American voters endorsed in the 1992 general election campaign. My proposals will freeze the rate of increase in demand for social services in less than five years and produce a major leap forward in the development of an American culture to cope with the freedom that technology, democracy, pluralism, secularism, and security from aggression have brought us.

1

Actuarial Arithmetic

Significant changes in American culture emerge from mass movements, and all mass movements depend on the stories we tell one another about who we are and what goals and values are important to us. The stories we are telling one another about family, work, and child care are basically wrong, but they are not wrong because Americans have become moral degenerates or more libido-driven and egocentric than other societies. America was the first society with enough money to concern itself with the pursuit of happiness for everyone—including ordinary workers—and to experience the technological revolution that made children useless economically while opening up market-sector jobs for women.

Such a profound technological revolution brought its blessings but also its peculiar problems. Preeminent among these problems is the looming collapse of the public sector caused by the bankruptcy of what we have come to think of as the "social safety net." The government social insurance system at both the federal and state levels cannot handle the massive transfer of family costs to public agencies that inadvertently has become the natural offshoot of the pursuit of happiness. Furthermore, the near-bankruptcy of governments like those of the states of California and New York is only the most conspicuous symptom of a far more extensive collapse that extends to the execrable education in our schools, the loss of jobs to more productive overseas competitors in our economy, and the burgeoning crime in our neighborhoods.

All of this has begun to happen, strangely enough, simply because American parents no longer need children in the same way that children were needed in the United States fifty years ago or are needed today in developing countries. Even as late as the end of World War II, 17 percent of Americans were farmers for whom children were indispensable to perform valuable work. Now, with less than 2 percent of

Americans farming, children no longer are needed to help adults in part-time jobs or to extend families through marriage to support parents in old age. Although we have hardly noticed it, American children are no longer an integral part of economic and social life and have become instead a major expense. From an economic point of view, children are a luxury that must be paid for with foregone opportunities to pursue happiness.

Over the past fifty years, the declining economic role of children engendered by industrialization has shrunk American families so that today's children not only have fewer brothers and sisters, but also a shortage of aunts, uncles, and cousins who might love, care for, and encourage them. And, with the high level of labor mobility that industrialization requires, children are increasingly unlikely to be raised anywhere close to their grandparents or collateral kin. Few people now have the diverse, extended family groups within which children's care was (and in many parts of the world still is) flexibly shared. Without a reliable Social Security Administration to see them through their old age, Chinese adults, for example, must rely on the loyalty and affection of their children.

At another level, women do not need men the way they once did. Heavy farm work is no longer an integral part of almost everyone's daily life, and there are no invading Vikings, roaming mercenary armies, or marauding Indians to make combative males valuable. Furthermore, women can perform the light work now demanded by most jobs. What Murphy Brown and the typical welfare mother have in common is that both can live and support a child without the aid of a man.

High-income parents can afford to hire good surrogates to care for their children. This, indeed, is what the fabled television character Murphy Brown does. Working-class parents with nearby relatives generous enough to babysit can also find good care. But as our rising crime and teenage pregnancy rates and our falling literacy rate amply demonstrate, children are routinely being left more and more to their own devices.

In October 1990, students at Washington's Bunker Hill Elementary School were asked by the *Washington Post* whether they were sometimes left home alone. Out of twenty-nine children—most of them seven years old—all but two raised their hands. Ten children in the group said that they used a key to let themselves into an empty house after they left school at 3 P.M. every day. One second-grader explained that even if he lost his key, he was small enough to go in through the doggie door.[1] Although parents usually comprehend the danger of these situations, they are caught between the need to work, the expense of child care, and the absence of relatives or friends who can supervise the children.

The high percentage of caretaker parents who work outside the home not only affects children within their own families—particularly when parents are exhausted by outside work—but also *communities* of children. Whole neighborhoods—most prominently middle-class neighborhoods—are now bereft of adult leadership during all the workday hours that children are home from school. This means that such leadership for children as exists in these neighborhoods comes from other children and not from parents.

Significantly, our experiences in providing social services have taught us that the early utopian socialists (like Edward Bellamy) were wrong. Communal facilities like day-care centers cannot care for children competently at lower per-unit costs than can poor or median-income stay-at-home parents. Although this proposition seems to defy what we think we know about economies of scale, the way government is organized and financed guarantees that viable public alternatives to family care can never be bought for what most Americans are willing to pay. This is because social programs with universal entitlement become so expensive that there is no opportunity to shift the cost from medium- and low-income families to upper-income families.

Throughout American society, there is a subliminal expectation that government will solve family-related problems through the inauguration of massive communal programs. Such life-saving programs on the enormous scale necessary to meet our needs are complete impossibilities, by which I mean real impossibilities, not just a selfish unwillingness on the part of upper-income taxpayers to help those in need.

Three counterintuitive political aspects of government finance must be mastered before one can adequately appreciate the impossibility of transferring private family costs to public budgets. The first is the way we buy goods though the public process, where the providers of government services end up being more important than the

---

1. *Washington Post,* 12 Oct. 1990, A1.

consumers of those services. The second is the difference between federal financing and state financing, including the natural limits to progressive taxation. And, the third is the difference between social insurance programs and social benefit programs because the two are now so hopelessly confused that even mayors, governors, and senators don't appreciate their crucial difference.

Buying goods through the public political process is both different and more expensive than buying the same goods privately. American electoral democracy has two components—voter numerosity and voter intensity. Although consumers of government services are numerous, they are not intense. It is the providers of government services who are intense, because their entire livelihoods depend on government largess. Provider intensity translates directly into political campaign contributions, organized election day support, and constant badgering from the providers' influential lobbyists. Public school teachers and service personnel, for example, have persuaded legislatures everywhere to enact mind-boggling seniority rights, irrational credential requirements, and restrictive work rules because there is no organized, counterbalancing parent and student lobby.

Some New York City public school janitors earn $70,000 a year in an educational system that combines teacherless classrooms with more school administrators than the whole of France. In 1988, New York City gave unionized janitors raises averaging $11,500 in exchange for permitting parents and teachers to conduct educational programs after school hours. Yet today, if a PTA wants to hold tutoring sessions or parenting classes that keep the school open beyond the contracted extra six hours a month, it must pay an additional $90 to a school janitor.[2] Almost half of the $7,080 per child that New York City spent in its public school system in fiscal 1992 was consumed in costs other than direct instruction—guidance and attendance counselors, maintenance workers, security guards, and other personnel as well as transportation and security.[3] This incredible administrative cost does less to enhance the quality of education than to provide thousands of high-paying jobs.

One reason, then, that a dream program like universal, publicly financed day care is impossible is its prohibitive expense. Inevitably,

2. See K. Boo, "The Worst City Government," *Washington Monthly* (Dec. 1990)
3. New York City Public Schools, *Vital Statistics: 1991-1992 School Year* (New York: Board of Education, 1992), 84.

day-care workers won't be just ordinary parents taking care of six children rather than one. Instead, day-care workers will end up being credentialed, organized, and, most of all, administered. Ostensibly the regulation will be to protect against child abuse and to assure that caretakers are sufficiently educated to expand the horizons of the children in their charge. These are laudable goals, but suddenly we are not just replacing the ordinary mom or pop, but improving upon her or him substantially. This is where the utopian socialists erred: They failed to comprehend that government will always be perverted to the maximum extent possible to serve the ends of government workers rather than government consumers. Liberals understand this proposition when it comes to the defense budget, but they seem baffled by it in other areas like day care and behavioral health services.

Counterintuitive as it may seem, the means invariably overwhelm the ends at all levels of government. Political battlefields are perennially littered with the mangled corpses of officials who believed government could be run like a business. But government and business run on completely different principles. Business thrives on efficiency, while government thrives on patronage. Business always lowers costs as a means to an end, while in government the means are the end. That's why the back-slapping, log-rolling, pork-barrelling, job-giving, vote-buying, and deal-making Dick Daleys (senior) and Alfonse D'Amatos of this world are so wildly successful in politics, while the narrow, clean-cut, honest, technocratic, humorless Michael Dukakises, Jerry Browns, and Richard Lamms are such stupendous failures.[4]

Notwithstanding all of the free-market rhetoric of the Reagan era, the longest peacetime boom in recorded history (1982–90) was fueled by the largest peacetime deficit in recorded history, much of which went into a massive defense build-up. Instead of the old Roosevelt "tax tax, spend spend, elect and elect," the stolid Republicans of the 1980s improved upon the New Deal vote buying formula with "borrow borrow, spend spend, elect and elect." And it worked

4. I am trying to explain these matters in simple, commonsense terms, but both Kenneth Arrow and James Buchanan have won separate Nobel Prizes for their work in "public choice theory." Public choice theory, as a subspecialty of economics, involves the construction of complex mathematical models to explain behavior that anyone who has ever been elected county commissioner or sheriff understands intuitively. See, for example, Kenneth Arrow, *Social Choices and Individual Values* (New York: John Wiley and Sons, 1951), and James Buchanan, *Essays on the Political Economy* (Honolulu: University of Hawaii Press, 1989).

for quite awhile, but only because Reaganomics was really Keynes as restated by Kafka. Having now stretched ourselves to the breaking point, however, only big tax hikes will give us more government programs. Roughly 6 percent of our gross national product (not our federal budget) is devoted simply to paying the interest on the national debt.

The ability of the federal government to borrow year after year, without any repayment, leads to the widespread conviction that taxes and expenditures are not firmly linked. Yet as the campaign rhetoric of both parties in 1992 clearly indicates, it has finally dawned on most Americans that continued 1980s-style deficits cannot be sustained. That, indeed, is what the (not terribly successful) bipartisan Gramm-Rudman-Hollings Act is all about, and Gramm-Rudman-Hollings means (whenever it is taken seriously) that federal programs cannot grow in the next decade without commensurate tax increases. Notably, the Clinton administration is busy attempting to raise taxes both to create new programs like univeral health care and to reduce the deficit.

Lots of plans have been made to spend the "peace dividend" on domestic programs, including public day care. But because the voters can understand most domestic programs, the voters can also understand that they would rather keep their money (or their indebtedness) in their own pockets than buy goods and services for others. Everybody, of course, has his or her own pet project, but the parents who want day care don't want to buy roads for truck drivers, and the highway contractors who are already well insured don't want to buy health insurance for low-income workers. Retired people want lower taxes rather than better schools, and no one who lives in a clean place wants to shell out the dollars to remove a toxic waste dump from someone else's back yard. After all, everything looks like a good idea until the person doing the looking is asked to pay the bill.

At this point, the beauty of national defense as a Keynesian, pork barrel employment generator enters the picture. Almost everyone believes that he or she needs at least a little national defense, yet happily the details of defense are so supremely boring that no one is willing to devote leisure hours to understanding the value of bombers over submarines or the specifications for antiballistic missile systems. Indeed, the greatest monument to the cooperative spirit that defense uniquely inspires is that our national education act and national highway act of 1950s vintage were named the "National Defense Education Act" and the "National Defense Highway Act," respectively. As Gramm-Rudman-Hollings clearly demonstrates, however, there is money for only one such massive Keynesian job-producing program, and that program will probably remain defense and not day care or any other family-substitute program.

Boldfaced political lies like "no new taxes" are prompted by the voters' desperate desire to believe in a cornucopia of government programs paid for by someone else. Government has the power to redistribute wealth, which means that it is at least theoretically possible to provide any selected group with benefits paid for by some other group. And, frequently, government does provide free benefits such as disability pensions, public housing, and public education to people who don't pay taxes. But there are severe limits to wealth redistribution through the tax system in a functioning democracy.

In general, federal programs are funded by more progressive taxes than state and local programs because the federal government raises most of its money—except the money to support social security and medicare—either by personal and corporate income taxes or by borrowing. State and local governments, on the other hand, have a lot of regressive taxes. State income taxes are usually progressive, but most other state taxes are either proportional—like the taxes on real estate— or downright regressive—like the sales taxes on food, liquor, beer, cigarettes, and gasoline. At the state and local levels, the linkage between programs and taxes is firm because, unlike the federal government, states, counties, and cities cannot borrow to support their operating (as opposed to capital) budgets, except, perhaps, on a short-term basis to meet casual deficits.[5] Indeed, state constitutions usually forbid deficit financing of operating budgets and require voter approval for any general obligation borrowing to finance roads or schools.

The two big federal programs that are progressively funded are

5. Casual deficits can, nonetheless, be significant, and the difference between operating budgets and capital improvements is not nearly as clear in practice as it is in theory. For example, notwithstanding that the State of New York has a provision in its constitution requiring a balanced budget, New York piled up a $5 billion deficit in 1990. Tax revenues were less than expected, and the state's welfare costs were soaring. Months of deadlock between the governor and the legislature over the budget were resolved only by a series of accounting gimmicks that included arranging for the state to "sell" some of its prisons and highways to itself and then issue bonds to pay for the purchase. In the process, New York's bond ratings became the third lowest in the country. See C. Mann, "The Prose (and Poetry) of Mario M. Cuomo," *The Atlantic* (Dec. 1990).

national defense and welfare. Welfare includes the federal portion of aid to families with dependent children (AFDC), the food stamp program, medicaid, social security supplemental income (SSI), and miscellaneous other need-based programs. The most important federal programs, however—social security and medicare—are funded by user fees. Everyone who works pays 7.65 percent of his or her wages up to a limit of $53,400 a year in social security payroll taxes, and the employer pays an equal amount.[6] The employer's share of social security taxes, of course, is money that is not available for wage payments, so in many industries the worker is actually giving up 15.3 percent of his or her wage fund to pay for social security and medicare. Among low-wage employees, the social security tax, which is levied on the first dollar earned, is significantly more burdensome than the progressive income tax, which allows a $2,150 exemption per household member plus numerous deductions and credits.

The largely regressive nature of state and local taxes is a constant irritant to everyone who works for state and local government and to the leaders of powerful labor and consumer lobbies. Consequently, state and local governments do not continue to use proportional or regressive taxes because elected officials oppose progressivity. Rather, our federal system of government imposes structural limits on any state's ability to tax progressively because rich people can easily leave high-tax states and go to low-tax states. This problem is far less pronounced in other industrial countries because cultural and language differences with neighboring countries make flight across national borders unattractive.

The most dangerous tax for an American state to impose is a confiscatory, progressive personal income tax because such a tax becomes so high a percentage of total fixed costs for the rich that the rich invariably leave. Higher income taxes can be imposed on the working class, however, because paying the taxes is still cheaper than moving. Ironically, therefore, what often begins as a progressive tax to tap the coffers of the rich ends up catching the middle and working classes in a regressive spiral that raises middle- and working-class taxes year after year. The way this works is that the initial

6. In addition, effective January 1991, a new tax of 1.45 percent was imposed on earnings between $53,400 and $125,000 to support medicare. This new tax has some progressive implications that the regular social security tax does not have, but this does not change the fact that social security and medicare are primarily funded by user fees.

targets of a confiscatory progressive income tax—the super-rich—leave in a year or two after the tax is enacted, but by the time they leave, programs are in place predicated upon the estimated taxes the rich would have paid had they stayed. These programs, then, can be sustained only by raising taxes once again, but this time on the upper-middle and middle classes. Then, as taxes for these groups rise, it becomes advantageous for the upper-middle and middle classes to leave as well. And so once again taxes must be raised, but this time on even lower-bracket taxpayers.

When executives move, they take their companies and their personal expenditures with them. All of this has already happened in New York. New Jersey officials are convinced that New York's extraordinarily high state and city personal income taxes have made New Jersey rich.[7] Companies have simply followed their chief executive officers across the Hudson River to New Jersey, where most of the benefits of the New York metropolitan area are available, but the taxes are about half. Similarly, Florida—a state without either an income tax or an estate tax—has become a mecca for the mobile elderly rich. In Florida, aging tycoons can escape the progressive income taxes of the Northeast (where they made their fortunes) and keep a higher percentage of their money for their heirs. Ironically, however, many aging tycoons rent houses in New York, Massachusetts, or Connecticut but make sure they spend barely more than six months each year in Florida. Thus, the high-tax northeastern states end up providing the Florida residents with services anyway but get no taxes except the sales tax in return.

Economists point out that the American federal system, which forces states to compete for plant locations and taxpaying residents just like private business must compete for customers, is one of the reasons that the United States has the lowest effective tax rate of any in-

7. In New York City, state and local taxes consume 17.8 percent of the gross city product (a measure of all goods and services produced in the city). For the rest of the nation, the state and local tax burden is only 9.5 percent of gross product. Despite the recession of 1992, the Dinkins administration in New York City and the State of New York continued to raise taxes, to the tune of $2.6 billion, in order to close the budget gap created by a stagnant economy. Two new charges on the city's personal income tax raised the top marginal rate from 3.4 to 4.46 percent. The city also imposed several hundred million dollars in new property taxes and did not implement some promised tax cuts. See S. Kagann, "New York's Vanishing Supply Side," *City Journal* (Autumn 1992).

dustrialized Western country.[8] Indeed, this low overall tax rate is one of the reasons that the United States has stayed more or less competitive in world markets notwithstanding that American industry gets much less help from the government and substantially fewer nontariff barriers to foreign competition than our European or Japanese trading partners.[9] But for those who would like to see a Swedish-style welfare state with universal public day care, the American federal system is a major obstacle because only the federal government can impose the necessary taxes. The old idea (made famous by Justice Louis D. Brandeis) that the states can be laboratories for social experiments is nice in theory, but in practice no state can afford to perform costly experiments for fear of losing industry, jobs, and tax bases when its taxes get out of line with those of neighboring states.

Nonetheless, if publicly funded day care or any other family substitute program had overwhelming popular support, it could be put in place by the federal government. At the height of the Great Depression, no state could afford unilaterally to burden its industry with unemployment insurance premiums. To solve this competitive problem, the Roosevelt administration imposed a federal tax on employers[10] unless a state levied its own tax to establish a state unemployment compensation system. If a state failed to act, the federal tax was simply paid into the Treasury without earmark, but if the state established a qualifying state unemployment insurance system, 90 percent of the state tax was a credit against the federal tax.

However, (and it's a big "however" for anyone who expects public day care or an augmentation in other family substitute programs) al-

8. See, for example, Mansur Olson, *The Rise and Decline of Nations* (New Haven: Yale University Press, 1982).

9. As of December 1990, the United States had an overall favorable balance of trade except in two important sectors—petroleum and automobiles. The decline in the value of the American dollar between 1985 and 1990, combined with improved efficiency among American producers, narrowed significantly the trade imbalance over what it had been just five years earlier. Indeed, a significant part of the 1990 trade deficit was directly related to the Iraqi invasion of Kuwait and the consequent increase in international oil prices.

10. Now levied under 26 *U.S.C* § 3301, *et seq.* Mr. Justice Cardozo pointed out in *Steward Machine Co. v. Davis,* 301 U.S. 548 (1937) (the case that pronounced the tax constitutional) that the purpose of the federal tax was to avoid differences in manufacturing costs among the states so that states would not be discouraged from inaugurating employment security programs from fear that their industries would be placed at a competitive disadvantage.

though the federal government discovered a way to mandate nation-wide unemployment insurance, the financing device was anything but progressive. All employers in the United States are charged an insurance premium to fund unemployment compensation. The premium rate varies depending on the employment experience of both the industry and the specific employer. Thus, notoriously cyclical industries like construction pay higher premiums than stable industries like public utilities. But even within the same industry, the employers who lay off or fire more workers than the industry norm pay higher premiums, while the employers who lay off or fire fewer workers than the industry norm pay lower premiums.

In unemployment compensation, because the entire tax is paid by the employer, the government appears to have created a free benefit. Workers suspect that if the government didn't require employers to pay unemployment insurance premiums, the employers would just pocket the money and spend it on fast horses, old whiskey, and wild parties. Although the Republicans have battalions of well-groomed, earnest young economists to prove that if money weren't being paid in unemployment insurance premiums it would be paid in wages or used to lower consumer prices, Democrats are convinced that unemployment insurance redistributes wealth from owners and managers to workers.

Unfortunately, labor economics is a surpassingly complicated subject, so how much of the cost of employer-paid-for benefits like unemployment compensation ends up coming out of the workers' and consumers' hides depends on a host of factors, including: (1) the labor-to-capital ratio of the industry; (2) the degree to which the industry is a monopoly or oligopoly; (3) the extent of international competition; and (4) the extent of unionization.[11] At the extremes, however, mini-

---

11. When Richard Nixon imposed wage-price controls in 1971 (which had the effect of freezing the wages of ordinary workers while leaving management's salaries and stockholders' dividends free to rise), I made a stab at sorting some of this out in a coherent way. Both conservative and middle-of-the-road economists argue that unions can't redistribute wealth from owners to workers by forcing up wages because rising wages will always reduce the total number of employees, thus reducing overall worker welfare. Indeed, these economists make a strong case that whenever wages rise, workers are laid off because (1) capital becomes cheaper relative to labor, which causes the substitution of capital for labor; and, (2) higher labor costs force prices to rise, which reduces the amount of end product bought by consumers. Much of this is correct sometimes, but exactly how it works—and whether it works at all—depends on factors I have

mum-wage employees working in car washes give up nothing from their wages for unemployment insurance, while unionized auto workers foot the whole bill because their union can squeeze management for the entire "wage fund." Therefore, low-wage workers gain when we force employers to pay for worker benefits like unemployment insurance while high-wage, unionized workers or nonunion, skilled craftsmen tend to pay a big part of the cost of the benefit themselves.

In contrast, indirect taxes like unemployment insurance premiums, workers' compensation premiums, road taxes on trucks, and property taxes on commercial and industrial property tend to have a severely regressive effect on working-class consumers. This regressive effect of hidden taxes partially explains the reduction in real private purchasing power from 1980 to the present among lower-middle- and working-class Americans. (Chapter 4 will discuss the other causes.) Indirect taxes comprise a fair percentage of the cost of necessities like food and transportation; what to the casual observer may look like free government benefits for the ordinary working stiff are actually paid for by the same working stiff at the supermarket check-out counter and the car dealer's showroom. Perhaps the best way to explain how this works is to explore what economists call "the great hamburger paradox."[12]

Let us ask ourselves why a hamburger and a beer at lunchtime in the garden dining room of New York's Plaza Hotel costs $40, while the exact same hamburger and beer somewhere off the interstate near Salina, Kansas, costs $5.50? The answer, of course, is that the Plaza has a lot of costs besides the cost of the food that need to be passed on to someone. At the Plaza, for instance, the table has a fresh linen cloth that must be laundered after each customer, and the waiter wears a tuxedo that must be dry-cleaned regularly. In Salina, our burger and beer are served at the counter, and the waitress doing the serving is dressed in a sweatshirt and jeans. Around the Plaza Hotel, ground-floor space costs about $250 a square foot per year, while comparable space in Salina costs $8. At the Plaza, all the cutlery is heavy silver plate and the glasses are cut crystal. In Salina, the knives, forks,

---

explained in detail in "Why Wage-Price Guidelines Failed: A 'Theory of the Second Best' Approach to Inflation Control," *West Virginia Law Review* 79 (1976): 1.

12. This term was invented by Albert T. Sommers of The Conference Board sometime in the 1970s, but neither he nor I can find the newsletter in which it was first used.

spoons, and glasses are like the ones the army piles by the hundreds at the entrance to chow lines. The waiter at the Plaza has a towel draped over his arm, calls you "Monsieur" or "Madame," and fawns over you; the waitress in Salina simply smiles and says, "Hi Hon, what's yours?"

In short, the quality of the meat, fries, lettuce, tomato, ketchup, and beer plays an insignificant role in the price difference between the Plaza Hotel and the Salina diner. What we are paying for at the Plaza has nothing to do with food and drink, but rather with a host of intangibles like physical location, atmosphere, and flattery.

The "atmosphere" that we buy when we lunch at the Plaza is exactly like the unemployment insurance, workers' compensation, and four-lane highways that we inadvertently buy when consumer prices rise to cover indirect taxes. Because politicians substitute indirect taxes for direct taxes whenever possible, each time we pay for some pedestrian good or service we are also paying for a host of government benefits. In politics—unlike business—the real world is the world of illusions, and indirect taxes nibble their way into our incomes with such tiny bites that they are barely noticeable. Upper-income taxpayers, including senators, congressmen, judges, state legislators, government executives, and all their social friends, prefer regressive indirect taxes to progressive direct taxes because indirect taxes raise most of their money from people who are not rich. Working people (who don't have Ivy League tax lawyers to explain these things to them in the comfort of their own homes) think of indirect taxes as taxes on "business." Everyone ends up happy, but as usual the working class takes a beating.

Much of the "inflation," then, that America has experienced since 1960 is not really inflation at all. Rather, prices have been going up in stores, restaurants, hospitals, garages, and resorts because we are buying more, much more. However, what we are buying are things like higher unemployment compensation benefits, greater health insurance coverage through state medicaid, bigger workers' compensation awards, four-lane highways, better school buildings, and even bigger jury awards in product liability and automobile accident suits. These valuable goods and services are entirely unrelated to the suit of clothes, car, or roast that we are consciously purchasing. Of course, we are also buying greater waste, utterly foolish projects, and bigger bureaucracies, but we are nonetheless buying something and, like having lunch at the Plaza, the somethings that we are buying are part and parcel of the "atmosphere" we take for granted rather than deliberate selections from the menu.[13]

The larger the program that government attempts to inaugurate (particularly something as massive as public day care), the smaller the extent to which the costs can be shifted from users to nonusers. And here it is important to distinguish social insurance programs from universal user programs. In social insurance, the government assesses a small premium on everyone for the benefit of a few people who are unlucky enough to get hit by a tragedy like giving birth to a retarded child. Social insurance is cheap because few people are unlucky enough to qualify for benefits. Other government programs, however, like social security or the public schools, are terribly expensive because everyone uses them. As I shall explain in the next chapter, programs that were once thought to fall into the social insurance category—like medicaid, foster care, and child protective services—have now hopelessly unraveled because the number of families that require the services are numerous beyond anything envisaged when the programs were set up. Rather than merely providing protection from the occasional family hardship, government is increasingly becoming a substitute for family.

This substitution does not come cheap. The fastest growing areas of state budgets, growing much faster than either state revenues or state budgets as a whole, are corrections, medicaid, welfare, and SSI/

---

13. A good example of how we pay for valuable things like a healthy environment emerges from the Clean Air Act of 1990. The act restricts sulfur dioxide emissions—considered to be the leading cause of acid rain—from coal-fired power plants. Thus, coal-fired plants, primarily located in the Midwest and the Ohio Valley, must cut their sulfur dioxide emissions by half, or nine million tons annually, in the next decade. The restrictions, which take effect in 1995 and tighten in 2000, essentially give power plants that now burn high-sulfur coal three options.

First, power plants can install scrubbers at a cost of up to $100 million each, which would eliminate as much as 90 percent of the sulfur emissions and allow the plants to continue to burn high-sulfur coal. Second, power plants can switch to low-sulfur coal (primarily from the West) and pay generally higher transportation costs. Third, power plants can trade or sell pollution allowances, permitting some plants to exceed standards to the extent other plants come in under the limits.

Nonetheless, whatever path a particular public utility now using high-sulfur coal chooses, its cost of producing electric power will increase, and that increase will necessarily be passed on to consumers. Is this inflation? Certainly not, because we are not just paying a higher price for the same old electricity. Rather, we are buying a new commodity, clean air.

SSP.[14] In California, the overall growth rate of the state budget was 8 percent over the last decade (between fiscal year 1983–84 and fiscal year 1993–94). During that period, the corrections budget grew at nearly twice the state growth rate (14 percent). The health (medicaid) and welfare (AFDC and SSI/SSP) portions of the California budget each grew at a rate of 10 percent. In New York, more money will be spent on medicaid in fiscal year 1993–94 than on education.[15] Indeed, this explosion of demand to substitute government services for family functions is the driving force behind New York's $6 billion 1992–93 budget gap[16] and California's $14.3 billion and $11.2 billion budget gaps in fiscal years 1991–92 and 1992–93, respectively.[17]

"Budget gaps" are not "deficits." Through a combination of cuts in services, blue smoke, and mirrors, California and New York theoretically spent no more than they took in. In order to prevent the "budget gaps" from becoming "deficits," however, the governments cut important existing services.[18] In California over the last decade, state spending on elementary and secondary education grew at a rate below that of the overall budget, while appropriations for higher education are

14. Although it may at first seem strange that corrections (i.e., prisons) are family substitutes, a direct correlation has been established between the breakdown of the family and increased juvenile and adult delinquency (chapters 2 and 5).

15. In fiscal year 1986-87, New York spent $6 billion on medicaid (state and federal money combined) and $7.7 billion on education. However, in fiscal year 1993-94, medicaid spending will outstrip education spending by $13.7 billion to $11.9 billion.

16. Governor of New York, "Message of the Governor for Fiscal Year 1992-93," *Executive Budget, Annual Message.*

17. California Legislative Analyst, *State Spending Plan for 1992* (Nov. 1992). Although California may have the most staggering budget gaps in terms of dollars, it has by far the largest population of any state. However, California is in no way unique in terms of the stresses being placed on its budget. Even in West Virginia, corrections, health, and welfare budget growth rates have exceeded the overall growth rate of the state budget. The "health and welfare" expenditures (primarily corrections, public assistance, and medicare) comprised 22 percent of the West Virginia budget in 1989; in 1992, "health and welfare" comprised a whopping 42 percent. West Virginia State Auditor, *Analysis of Receipts and Expenditures* (1989, 1992).

18. Nationally, "[m]edicaid has increased to 17 percent of state spending [not counting the federal share] in fiscal 1992 from 10 percent in fiscal 1987. Spending for elementary and secondary education has decreased to 21 percent in fiscal 1992 from 23 percent in fiscal 1987. Similarly, higher education spending has decreased slightly to 11.5 percent in fiscal 1992 from 12.0 percent in fiscal 1987; this is largely because of increases in tuition and fees. Essentially, these shifts confirm the Governors' concerns that the rising cost of health care is reducing the share of state spending going to education and other long-term investments. This is not a healthy long-term trend." National Governors' Association, *The Fiscal Survey of States: April 1993,* 8.

projected to be cut by 10 percent in real dollars in fiscal year 1993–94.[19] Police protection, fire protection, road maintenance, and other traditional, desirable, valuable local government services have all had their budgets cut to prevent the state governments from running actual deficits. Given the limited potential for states to increase their revenues significantly in the near future, the decision of which services are provided by the states has increasingly become a zero-sum game.

After-school child monitoring and preschool infant day care are both valuable services that we can either buy with our own money or convince the government to buy for us with someone else's money. Given the choice, most of us would prefer the latter. In the language of economists, the elusive but fabled "rational consumer" will substitute communally bought goods for privately bought goods whenever possible. Therefore, once child care becomes publicly funded, many parents who now stay home to care for their own children will seek outside employment because they are going to be paying for child care regardless of whether they use it. Other parents who currently pay for their own child care would end up paying for public day care they won't be able to use because in many places public care would be of dangerously low quality. This, then, is the central focus of objections to public day care.

Those who currently take care of their own children (1) themselves, (2) through relatives like grandparents, or (3) through hiring someone they know to be reliable don't want to pay heavy additional taxes for incompetent, dangerous, disease-ridden public day care that they don't expect to be able to use. The response to these objections

19. California has moved to tap user fees and property taxes to pay for services once funded by the state general fund. California increased the proportion of property taxes used to fund public schools, thus reducing the remaining money available to localities to fund police, fire protection, pothole filling, and other services provided by localities. National Governor's Association, *The Fiscal Survey of States: April 1993,* 17. Proposition 13 has limited the ability of California to raise property taxes; ultimately the substitution of government services for private family investment (both in terms of money and of time) is being paid for by cuts in traditional local government services.

To make up for the cuts in the higher education budget, tuition and fees at public institutions have been raised significantly. The University of California and California State University systems nearly doubled their tuitions between 1991 and 1993, while California community colleges tripled their tuition during that same period. California Legislative Analyst, *State Spending Plan for 1992* (Nov. 1992). The University of California System, which used to pride itself on providing low-cost quality college education, is increasingly shedding that low-cost image (as well, perhaps, as some of the quality).

by those who dream of a system like Sweden's with universal, publicly funded day care is that no one is talking about "poor quality" day care. The retort by those who oppose public day care is that nothing we are currently doing in the public sector should lead us reasonably to believe that a real (rather than imagined) public program will be "good" public day care.

If public day care were implemented, it is doubtful whether a majority of the women whose children are below school age and who now stay home would continue to do so regardless of the public program's quality. If working-class tax rates rise by 15 percent to pay for high quality public day care—something on a par with the public day care offered in Sweden—a sizable number of two-parent, single-earner families will have no choice but to become double-earner families just to pay the taxes. This, in fact, is what has happened in Sweden, where good quality day care is universally available but every parent—except, perhaps the super-rich—works.[20]

According to the 1990 census, roughly 40 percent of mothers with preschool children still stay home. With some families this is purely a philosophical choice,[21] but with many others it is just as purely an economic calculation. Nonetheless, as I shall demonstrate in chapter 4, stay-at-home mothers of preschoolers are making a gigantic contribution to this society, regardless of the reason that they have chosen to stay home.

Unskilled mothers who worked at the Seven-Eleven store before they had children simply can't earn high enough wages to make outside work profitable when day-care costs are added to taxes, transportation, clothes, and out-of-home meals. Publicly funded day care, how-

---

20. I sometimes ski in the Alps with Swedes who flock to middle-class resorts like Chamonix and Zermatt. Invariably, when I ask about day care I get the same response: Public day care in Sweden is of acceptable quality, but the taxes that support it are so high that only super-rich families can afford not to have both parents work. For example, Marie Gip from Stockholm, who is a primary school teacher herself, says that she would like to stay home with her preschool children, but taxes are so high that even though her husband is an upper-middle-class executive she has no choice but to work.

21. Several years ago one of my friends resigned her partnership in a prestigious Charleston law firm when her first child was born. My friend, a graduate of Wellesley College and Boston University Law School, was married to a successful Harvard Business School graduate. She had always been a dedicated feminist and could have afforded high-quality child care had she chosen to continue working. She believed, however, that her children were more important than any extra income she could earn, and she thought she would be a better parent than anyone she could possibly hire to replace her at any price.

ever, would dramatically change these calculations and drastically increase overall demand for day care. Furthermore, many children who are currently cared for by close relatives for free would be shifted to a public program if one were available, and the likely effects of that shift would be to expose even more children to early and extensive low-quality day care.

It is axiomatic that when a commodity or service is provided free of charge, it is in everyone's interest to get as much of it as possible. Consequently, if the commodity or service has any value at all, it must be rationed in some way, and if no rational, explicit rationing system is put in place, the commodity or service will be rationed by natural mechanisms. In government, the most common natural rationing mechanism is general deterioration in the quality of the public good or service offered. For example, as widespread inner-city drug use has increased drug-related health problems like AIDS and crack addiction in newborn infants, inner-city public hospitals have simply fallen apart. The demand for expensive medical treatment so exceeds the supply that patients must wait for hours and then either don't receive treatment at all or receive only partial treatment.[22]

Demand for public goods of every description—hospitals, prisons, public housing, education, medical research—so outstrips society's resources that even if we taxed away all family income over $100,000 a year and confiscated all private wealth over $500,000 per couple, we still could not meet even the goals adumbrated in the 1992 Democrat party platform on a sustained basis.

For example, roughly thirty-seven million Americans are without health insurance. The uninsured are usually in higher-risk categories than the insured. The uninsured are more likely to smoke and be drug and/or alcohol abusers; they are more likely to have preexisting medical problems; and they are more likely to live under conditions that produce above-average health hazards—everything from gunshot wounds to AIDS. A need-based, national health insurance program would have high administrative costs, but even taking the most optimistic view possible and assuming that adequate health coverage could be bought for everyone not currently insured for $150 a month per person (only slightly more than what private employers and the

---

22. See "Public Hospitals Are Overloaded, Survey Shows," *Wall Street Journal*, 30 Jan. 1991, B3.

government are now paying for group health), the bill the first year would be at least $55.5 billion. And, if we include a dental care program, costs increase by at least $530 annually for each covered family.

The people advocating health insurance for the currently uninsured make a compelling case for wealth redistribution because all other developed Western countries have some type of guaranteed national health insurance.[23] Yet a compelling case also can be made for better public housing, more drug treatment facilities, and more $28,000-a-year prison beds. Add in help for our growing AIDS-infected population and for the multiply-handicapped children born to drug-addicted mothers, and it is clear that little money is left for such pedestrian concerns as repairing the infrastructure of cities, building energy-efficient mass transit systems, and cleaning up the environment.

Indeed, we could do any one of the things that I have just mentioned—starting with publicly funded, need-based health insurance—and fund the program through taxes on the richest 10 percent of the population. But we cannot do everything. And at this point it is open to doubt whether we *will* do anything. In 1988, Congress attempted to add catastrophic health insurance to medicare. The plan was funded by a severely progressive tax on the wealthiest social security recipients, but some additional payment was required of every retiree who was not abjectly poor. Wealthy retirees, however, already had private supplemental health insurance to pay for catastrophic illness, so they were outraged when they were taxed to provide expanded public coverage for others.

Rich retirees understood just how much they were paying and that

---

23. Ironically, those without insurance in the United States are not the very poor. Indeed, families qualified for aid to families with dependent children (welfare) receive a medicaid card entitling them to government-paid health care for themselves and their children. But as soon as a poor breadwinner pulls herself up far enough to go off welfare, but without landing a job that includes health insurance, she finds her family completely uninsured. The design of the system is so bad that even right-wing conservatives can't fault families for finding that welfare is more sensible than working. Our current system has such an idiotic design that millions of women work as household day laborers for cash payments while the government turns a blind eye—almost a conspicuous policy of nonenforcement. The government has never figured out how explicitly to permit some families to earn enough money to get them out of poverty and yet retain a medicaid card without encouraging rampant overuse of the system. Therefore, the conspicuous policy of nonenforcement becomes a pragmatic solution to an impossible rationing problem.

they were paying much more in taxes than private insurance would cost; middle-class retirees understood that they were paying higher premiums but didn't quite appreciate how valuable the benefits were. Finally, poor retirees—as is usual in these matters—didn't understand anything and weren't well enough organized to overcome the strong opposition of conservative lobbies dominated by upper-income retirees. So, in 1989—just a year after having passed the catastrophic health insurance program—Congress completely abolished the program.

There is a moral in the catastrophic health insurance story for those who want public day care and the augmentation of other family substitute programs. It is fairly clear that many of the middle-income retirees who supported repeal of catastrophic health insurance were in favor of the benefits but simply resented the taxes. Consequently, these retirees—at least at some unconscious level—really expected Congress to repeal only the increased taxes, leaving the benefits to be funded from general revenue. But catastrophic health insurance is far too expensive to be funded by further deficit financing, and Congress was loath to increase individual or corporate income tax rates. Thus the hope of free benefits on the part of beneficiaries who were asked to pay a little (but less than actual cost) kept there from being any benefits at all.

Perhaps the reason that so many people expect public day care is that the success of real insurance programs like unemployment compensation and social security led us to try more ambitious schemes that never were, and could never be, actuarially sound.[24] This is because social insurance can work only when programs are limited to protecting people from hardships not of their own making—like dying, getting old, or getting laid off. An underlying theme of this book is that social insurance must be like homeowners' fire insurance, which works because people avoid burning down their own houses. If people thought the easy way to change neighborhoods or refurbish their houses was to be cavalier about turning off the stove, the whole fire insurance industry would go bankrupt.

24. Unemployment compensation and social security are based on simple actuarial principles. Unemployment compensation is based on the principle that we can charge employers a premium to support laid-off workers for short periods. Social security is based on the principle that we can charge the younger working generation to support the older retired generation and that, when everyone pays 15.3 percent of the wage fund, we can all be protected against disability and the death of a wage-earner with dependent children. In unemployment compensation and social security, however, the charges are more or less actuarially sound.

This leads us, then, to another paradox, namely "the taking in one another's washing" paradox. If, for example, one head of household is killed in a mine disaster in a small town, his widow and children can survive by taking in other peoples' washing. Households that were perfectly happy to do their own washing before the tragedy will send their dress clothes to the Widow Smith so that she'll have honest work. But, if depression comes to the whole town because the local mine closes, the whole town can't survive by taking in one another's washing.

The most primitive form of social insurance involves the Widow Smith doing other people's washing after the tragic death of her husband. And if we play with that example for a moment we can illuminate some of the prerequisites for a politically and actuarially acceptable social insurance scheme. Let us, then, go back to the Widow Smith, but now, instead of assuming that she is a widow, let us assume that she is divorced or abandoned.

The economic effect on Mrs. Smith is the same whether the loss of her husband occurs through divorce, abandonment, or death, but the community's willingness to send her their washing will differ subtly depending on the cause of her penury. The reason for the difference is actuarial: We know that all husbands will strenuously avoid being killed, so we also know that the number of widows demanding our charity will be comparatively small. Divorce, however, doesn't discourage high risk behavior quite the way death does, so we could spend a lot of money supporting divorcées.

Consequently, other than accidental death, the strongest community impulse to charity for the Smith family will emerge if Mrs. Smith has been a dutiful wife who was abandoned by a loutish, no-account, drunken husband. And, even if Mrs. Smith divorced her husband, she will still elicit charity if Mr. Smith was brutal and profligate. But if Mrs. Smith divorced Mr. Smith because his conversation was tedious and his bedroom performance unimaginative, the community will extend little charity. After all, lots of other women find their husbands tedious as conversationalists and unimaginative as bed partners but stay married nonetheless.

Crude as this analysis may be, it seems to apply to most social problems—stretching all the way from AIDS to substance abuse. AIDS patients who have contracted AIDS through blood transfusions receive willing and even generous public support; those who contracted AIDS through high risk behavior such as sharing drug needles or engaging in unprotected sex receive only grudging support. And, notwithstanding the social service professionals' cries for more drug and alcohol treatment, taxpayer enthusiasm for funding expensive clinics is limited because both drinking and taking drugs are perceived by nonaddicts as voluntary acts.

We all know, of course, that not everyone can resist alcohol and drugs. But once we accede in a general way to the proposition that people are not responsible moral agents, everything from the criminal law to employer-employee relations falls hopelessly apart. Consequently, we are usually parsimonious about programs designed to relieve people from the consequences of their own voluntary acts.[25]

More important, however, there is an actuarial limit to our ability to rescue people from the consequences of their own voluntary acts. If a social insurance program changes behavior so that more people have "insured" losses, that social insurance program will either fail through deterioration of the product (like public hospital services) provided by the program or the program will turn into a prohibitively expensive universal-user program. That is why we have never attempted long-term unemployment insurance. Indeed, the duration of unemployment insurance is directly proportionate to the length of previous employment, and unemployment insurance also has a provision that severely penalizes workers who either quit their employers voluntarily or are discharged for misconduct.[26] Were it not for these limited barriers to overuse, unemployment insurance would become a vacation enhancement program.

25. Most students are shocked when they first read Thomas Malthus's theory of population growth—population grows geometrically, whereas food production grows arithmetically—and his admonition that helping the poor will only keep them alive to bring more poor, starving people into the world. Nonetheless, the United States has basically followed Malthusian principles in its dealings with the starving third world. Although the United States is generous with food relief in times of unexpected famine, flood, or earthquake, it is reluctant to provide food on a long-term basis to countries unable to feed their own populations. Basically, we have followed the old Quaker rule of "fishhooks but no fish." The United States has been willing to provide agricultural technology, training, and even credit for rural cooperatives—all things designed to help people grow their own food—but we have been unwilling to accede to requests for the long-term delivery of surplus agricultural products, even when the surplus is rotting in our warehouses. Although this seems heartless, the policy is necessary to encourage appropriate population control measures in third world countries and to avoid creating geometrically expanding populations entirely dependent upon American food for continued survival.

26. Typically, a worker who quits his or her employer voluntarily, or is discharged for misconduct, is disqualified from receiving unemployment benefits for six weeks, and a worker who is discharged for gross misconduct is disqualified indefinitely.

The problem of insureds voluntarily triggering their own losses that is pervasive in unemployment insurance potentially exists in most other social programs, which is why so few of them stay within budget and function properly. For example, latchkey children are the product of long-term but voluntary economic and social decisions. This may seem harsh, but birth control makes bringing children into the world whom one cannot support a voluntary act, unlike, for example, giving birth to a retarded child. The better any program for latchkey children becomes, the more parents will avail themselves of the program.

A good program for latchkey children, then, will cause more children to become latchkey. That means, in turn, that either the program will become progressively more expensive or the quality will deteriorate to such an extent that only the most desperate parents will use it. We may decide to support programs for latchkey children because, given the number of such children out there now without any supervision, doing so is the lesser of two evils. However, when we inaugurate such a program, we must understand that it will change private calculations to increase dependence on the program and expand it beyond simply caring for the children who are already in need.

In every decade since the 1950s the level of female labor force participation has risen. In 1991, 67 percent of all women with minor children worked outside the home, whereas in 1975 only 45 percent of women with minor children worked—a spectacular 22 percent increase in just fifteen years.[27] Furthermore, there has been no significant increase in the number of fathers staying home with their children. We now know that a legion of bad things directly related to the

27. Moreover, 60 percent of mothers with preschool-aged children work today, whereas only 37 percent of such mothers worked in 1975 (Table 621, *Statistical Abstract of the United States,* 1992). It seems counterintuitive that the female labor force participation rate for women with children—69 percent—would be higher than the national average of women as a whole—57.3 percent. However, there are several contributing factors to this phenomenon. Women over forty-five grew up at a time when women were encouraged to be full-time homemakers. Furthermore, young, single mothers usually must work if they wish their standard of living to be over poverty level, and young women today, unlike their elder sisters, have always expected to work.

A higher proportion of women with children work today than women without children. Nearly 75 percent of married women with school-aged children work, and 65 percent of single women with school-aged children work, while only 51 percent of married women without children work. This trend is probably symptomatic of the financial burdens children place on married couples.

decline in one-on-one, parent-child care have begun to happen,[28] and it is inconceivable that any type of public day care will be put in place in the next decade to reverse these trends.

Extensive studies of good child-care facilities by feminists like Deborah Fallows[29] reveal that even good to excellent hired day-care workers can't teach, encourage, and socialize children the way natural parents can. This means that our attempts to transfer private child-rearing costs to public agencies is not only economically and politically impossible, but it is also a very bad idea, even though we didn't know that it was a bad idea back when we decided to make the pursuit of happiness a reality for everyone.

Exactly how bad an idea it is to attempt to transfer private child-rearing costs to public agencies will become apparent in succeeding chapters where I show that whenever the transfer to public agencies is made, that transfer involves a net cost increase and a net quality decrease. Indeed, the next chapter will demonstrate that the social insurance safety net that we think we have been improving upon since World War II is actually an illusion, and its virtual collapse is inevitable unless we change our private behavior dramatically.

28. For example, since 1960 the following have occurred: violent crime has risen 560 percent; out-of-wedlock births have risen 400 percent; children in single-parent homes have tripled; and college-entry SAT scores have dropped nearly eighty points on average, even as the test was altered to remove cultural and racial biases against minorities; and teenage suicides have doubled. See William J. Bennett, *The Index of Leading Cultural Indicators* (Washington, D.C.: Empower America, The Heritage Foundation, and Free Congress Foundation, 1993).

29. Deborah Fallows, *A Mother's Work* (Boston: Houghton Mifflin, 1985).

2

The Safety Net Collapse

John Maynard Keynes's observation that in the long-run we are all dead has always had significant practical implications. It is easy for those who are warm, comfortable, and prosperous to prescribe short-term pain for others in pursuit of a better "long run." Most of the time, however, the future problems that professional alarmists wring their hands over are not the problems we actually face in the future, so we usually tell anybody who vaguely resembles Chicken Little to take a hike.

Occasionally, however, the long-run consequences of current actions are so inevitable that everyone comfortably may endorse tough cures. Take, for example, air and water pollution—problems that would have severely compromised living in America but for timely intervention. The current problems of illegitimacy, divorce, and lack of parental nurturing are similar to pollution problems because their consequences are so thoroughly exhausting our social insurance programs that the complete collapse of those programs is imminent. New York State's $6 billion budget gaps in 1991–92 and in 1992–93 and California's $11.2 and 14.3 billion budget gaps in 1991–92 and 1992–93[1] (leaving California to issue IOUs in lieu of checks for more than sixty days) represent the most dramatic examples of an impending financial collapse that threatens all urban states. Meanwhile, back in Washington, in the face of Gramm-Rudman-Hollings, the Congress consigns ever more responsibilities to the states, which in turn pass them on to counties and cities—something known as "shift and shaft" federalism.

Everywhere state and local governments are resorting to the tried and true budget balancing techniques of greater efficiency, reduced

1. See chapter 1, notes 15, 16.

services, and higher taxes. These techniques no longer work in urban states. As California governor Pete Wilson pointed out in 1991, you could lay off every California state employee, close down every California university, and open the gates to every California prison and still not balance the California budget. Indeed, California's 1992-93 budget gap of $14 billion-plus exceeded the total general revenue budgets of all but four of California's sister states.

The objective of this chapter is to bring home the fact that no tax increase, regardless of amount, can solve our problems without a simultaneous change in private behavior. Our existing social programs are rupturing because government can't fund the increasing number of claimants eligible for benefits. In constant dollars, welfare payments are only about 75 percent of what they were a decade ago, while medicaid reimbursements have fallen so low that unprecedented numbers of doctors are abandoning inner-city and rural practices. The flight of doctors from the rural areas of my home state in 1991, for example, compelled the West Virginia University medical schools to assume much of the responsibility for delivering health services to West Virginia's rural residents.

The year 1991 was particularly bad for welfare recipients almost everywhere in the United States. Nine states reduced benefits under the Aid to Families with Dependent Children program (AFDC), thirty-one froze benefits, and fourteen states cut and another thirteen froze general cash assistance payments—the program for poor people not eligible for AFDC.[2] By June 1993, in response to the welfare rolls exceeding five million AFDC families nationally, an all-time high, three states—Vermont, Florida, and Wisconsin—began a program gradually to limit welfare eligibility to roughly two years.[3]

The more than one million children who run away from home each year become involved in crime, drug networks, and prostitution, primarily to establish social ties.[4] Ultimately, most of these children get picked up on some public budget for at least a short time, effectively transferring private child-rearing costs of parents to the public sector.

2. See D. J. Besharov and Karen Baehler, "The Perverse Federal Incentives for Welfare Cuts," *Governing* (Feb. 1993): 11.

3. See Jason Deparle, New York Times Service, 2 June 1993, reprinted in the *Charleston Gazette*, 2 June 1993, 1A.

4. See J. P. Comer, "Kids on the Run," *Parents* (Jan. 1988).

Indeed, all public agencies—welfare departments, police departments, and the public schools—are crumbling under the burden of acting as surrogate parents to millions of children.

Social insurance is financed by everyone's paying a small premium to protect against unavoidable random tragedy. However, when tragedies are by and large avoidable, and such avoidable tragedies are rampant, the whole foundation on which social insurance is constructed breaks down both actuarially and politically. The political breakdown comes in the form of taxpayer revolt—the consistent election of anti-taxation candidates like Ronald Reagan and George Bush, or the passage of state tax limitation constitutional amendments like California's Proposition 13. Even in the 1992 presidential campaign, democrat Bill Clinton promised over and over again to give the middle-class a tax cut and to raise taxes only on the rich, defined as households making more than $200,000 a year. Had President Clinton told the truth about government's dire need for money, he, much like Walter Mondale in 1984, would have gone down in flames.

In short, demand for social services skyrockets while appropriations remain stagnant. Take prisons, for example. Presumably, everyone—liberals who want rehabilitation and conservatives who want to dump felons down a modern oubliette—would find prisons a high priority. As of 1989, however, thirty-six states were under court orders to relieve prison overcrowding.[5] We require new prison beds at the

5. After years of efforts by the judiciary in West Virginia to encourage the executive branch to take prison reform seriously, the West Virginia Supreme Court of Appeals finally declared in December 1988 that the conditions at Moundsville Penitentiary—the maximum security prison—were so substandard that the prison would be closed in 1992 regardless of whether there was another prison to take its place. However, to ensure that a new prison would be built, the court decided, in a related case, that the state constitution's requirement that voters approve all general revenue bond issues would not apply to bonds issued to build a prison. This holding was based on two considerations: first, voters would never approve a bond issue to build a prison; and second, the current prison did not meet federal standards under the U.S. Constitution's Eighth Amendment.

The conclusion that voter approval was not necessary for the issuance of bonds to build a prison followed from something known as the supremacy doctrine: Federal law supersedes all conflicting state law, and the limitation on bond issues, requiring, as it does, voter approval, would inevitably prevent the state from meeting federal prison standards. A more conservative judicial approach would have been simply to order the prison closed on a particular date and let the executive branch and the voters sort the problem out as best they could. However, practical experience instructed the court that when the date for closing came, there would be no facility to receive the prisoners, and

rate of one thousand every week, yet taxpayers won't pay. The furlough and work-release programs that Willie Horton symbolized in 1988, far from the product of woolly-headed liberals or weak-kneed judges, are in fact solely budget-driven.

If taxpayers won't pay to keep rapists and robbers out of their living rooms, why should anyone believe that taxpayers will pay to support foundlings, build public housing, or develop high-quality public day-care facilities? What government pretends to do and what government actually does are two entirely different matters, as our failure to appropriate enough money to punish felons proves. Often when we find a problem—like abandoned or neglected children—we create a government agency to solve the problem. We give the agency we create a lot of responsibility on paper but seldom appropriate an adequate amount of money.

For example, data from just about everywhere indicates that public foster care—the program that attempts to care for abused and neglected children—is an unmitigated disaster. Foster care children typically move several times a year and receive much less schooling than children in normal family settings. Well over 50 percent of all children in long-term foster care are functionally illiterate, and most suffer from low self-esteem, severe emotional disorders, and have limited opportunities for employment.[6] Very soon we are going to have about two hundred thousand children a year maturing into the adult population and will need to either support or incarcerate them all their lives.[7]

We stubbornly persist in creating social programs we know will fail because we cannot come to grips with our real problem—private irresponsibility. Our reluctance to prescribe a private morality arose in

---

the court would be confronted with a choice between backing down or releasing murderers, rapists, and robbers upon an unsuspecting world.

6. For a graphic description of the Kafkaesque child welfare bureaucracy, see "Robert's Journey Through the Children's Services Systems: A Case Study of Child Victimization," unpublished report to the West Virginia Supreme Court of Appeals by the West Virginia Juvenile Justice Committee, 2 April 1992, available through the Administrative Office of State Courts, Charleston, W.V.

7. This is a rough estimate based on the fact that in 1993 there were about 475,000 children in foster care—more than double the number of a decade earlier. I assume severe pathologies among slightly more than 40 percent, probably an optimistic estimate. The full ramifications of our foster care system are obscure to the general public because widespread foster care began only in the late seventies. Consequently, most foster care casualties are still children and hidden within the system.

the 1960s on the demise of the old consensus on race relations, sex roles, and relative power positions. Deeming the old consensus unjust to specific, identifiable groups—blacks, women, gays, children, and workers—the sixties generation agreed that the old consensus should be destroyed but reached no accord on a new counterconsensus. Because diverse groups seeking to change the existing consensus needed to work together, extreme tolerance was substituted for fixed standards. Being "nonjudgmental" was considered the politically correct stance on matters of private morality, and a live-and-let-live attitude about family arrangements or the lack thereof was one's ticket into the community of "progressive" leaders. Even Catholic politicians like Geraldine Ferraro and Mario Cuomo have scrupulously unburdened themselves of straight-laced Catholic morals in their public lives.

If America today is becoming miserly and mean-spirited in its programs for the poor, however, it is exactly because nonjudgmental media pundits, academicians, and politicians resist admitting the obvious: A pregnant fourteen-year-old and her irresponsible boyfriend bear no resemblance to other medicaid users—for example, the young working adult who contracts multiple sclerosis or the struggling couple whose child has cancer. These latter medicaid users are legitimate recipients of actuarially sound social insurance benefits because their medical tragedies are beyond their own control. The pregnant fourteen-year-old and her boyfriend, on the other hand, have created a public problem through their own private irresponsible behavior. To point out that the child of such a couple is innocent is morally sound but politically idiotic.

A comparison of social services expenditures with their speculative returns to other needed expenditures reveals the futility of demanding more social program money. Economists have documented the strong correlation between physical infrastructure—roads, bridges, airports, railroads, public utilities—and economic growth. The Associated General Contractors of America estimate that the necessary repairs and improvements to America's infrastructure will cost $3.3 trillion between 1991 and 2010. This figure is just slightly more than the total national debt in 1993, and even if we were to reduce this estimate by two-thirds in deference to the contractors' personal interest, the money needed is still staggering. Sixty percent of our nation's highways need work, ranging from repaving to major structural rehabilitation. In Massachusetts, the Department of Public Works currently strings nets under decayed overpasses to catch the concrete as it shears off.[8] Furthermore, in terms of political return, building infrastructure creates working-class jobs for the unskilled, while most social service jobs are for college graduates.

In 1990, New York City announced that it would reduce planned spending on bridge repairs from $1.2 billion to $930 million, effectively postponing work on some bridges until after 1992, even if it meant closing them in the meantime. Problems like this simply underscore the unavailability of new tax money for social services, which means that other projects must fund social services. Eventually, of course, highway users, education users (particularly after the savaging education took in California in the 1992–93 budget donnybrook), and public transport users will revolt against the reallocation of money and let the current social service system deteriorate from overuse so that social service clients simply die.

The federal government's continued ability to borrow has disguised the fact that it has been in worse shape than the states since 1987.[9] The collapse of the savings and loan industry led the federal government to assume $3 hundred billion in private liabilities, leaving the Resolution Trust Corporation the largest property owner in the United States. When the Pension Benefit Guaranty Corporation, the government agency that guarantees private pensions, demands billions of dollars to cover the junk bonds likely to go into default in the next decade due to looming private-sector bankruptcies, the federal government again may be compelled to meet a guarantee. And, if we have a severe recession in the mid-1990s, sorely underfunded unemployment insurance will require infusions of billions of additional dollars. In short, the federal government has nothing to spare to help the states.

And that, then, brings us to the stories that we tell one another about who we are, where we are going, and how we should live. Widely shared views of common problems are the product of the stories we tell one another, so if what we are doing doesn't work, we must first change the stories we are telling before we can change the way we do things. Indeed, the successful environmental and antismoking movements did not begin with programs and money but with a fundamental shift in the daily story line.

8. See J. Sedgwich, "Strong but Sensitive," *The Atlantic* (April 1991).
9. In 1993, interest on the national debt was roughly equal to all money expended for national defense.

The environmental and antismoking movements were really about what economists call "externalities."[10] The manufacturers who polluted the air and water passed a cost inherent in their for-profit manufacturing processes on to the rest of us, who were then expected either to put up with acid rain, dirty air, and dirty water or fork out our own money to abate those nuisances. Before the new environmental laws, manufacturers were allowed to "externalize" their costs by making other people pay costs that were properly the manufacturers'. Deferring environmental costs in the nineteenth century and the first half of the twentieth century by allowing nature to absorb pollutants permitted the United States to accumulate industrial capital quickly,[11] but as we became more crowded we could no longer rely upon nature's resilience alone. Because A does not want to pay to clean up B's mess, we have spent the years since the early seventies ending externalization to make B and B's customers pay for their own mess.

Likewise, a policy of amiable tolerance toward smoking despite widespread reports of its harmfulness was until quite recently the norm. Our laissez-faire morality dictated the nonjudgmental attitude that it was, after all, the smoker's life. Eventually, we came to understand that smokers not only jeopardize their own health, but also the health of everyone else. Smokers pollute indoor air, making it unpleasant and, perhaps, hazardous for nonsmokers; smokers increase medicare and medicaid costs; smokers use scarce hospital beds when treated for smoking-related diseases; and smokers often die young, leaving dependents for the rest of us to support. In short, smokers "externalize" their smoking-related costs.

Our new approach to smoking weighs the individual's right to make a private decision against that decision's harm to society. The

10. The classic treatment of externalities may be found in R. H. Coase, "The Problem of Social Cost," *Journal of Law and Economics* 3 (1960): 1. In general, I abhor professional jargon, but because the word *externality* is so concise, while plain-English substitutes like *privately unaccounted for enterprise costs* are so cumbersome, I shall use this jargon term and beg the reader's indulgence.

11. Third world countries never tire of pointing this out to us when we ask for international cooperation on environmental matters. Underdeveloped nations maintain that without the deferment of environmental costs, they cannot develop at an acceptable pace. Historically, this is a reasonable position, and it implies that if the developed countries want the third world to abate pollution at the same time that they develop themselves to first world standards, then the developed countries must share the cost of the environmental charges. Given our other budget problems, the likelihood of this happening is vanishingly small, so the world environment will deteriorate rather substantially in the next century.

result is that we discourage smoking without forbidding it. Although we have yet to promise smokers a public flogging, in many places the lives of smokers are made pretty miserable. Indeed, in some parts of the United States smoking is perceived as a social disease.

How we view illegitimacy, divorce, and two-earner couples too busy to care for their children must ultimately imitate how we have come to view smoking. Studies show that virtually everyone—man, woman, boy or girl—who conceives an illegitimate child understands the rudimentary mechanics of birth control, so society's problem is not sex "education." In fact, analysis by the Centers for Disease Control found students exposed to sex education to be slightly more likely to use birth control, but also slightly more likely to have sex at a younger age. The Centers for Disease Control found no difference in the pregnancy rate between those who had sex education and those who did not.[12]

One of the tacit assumptions of the social services lobby is that eventually things will get so bad that the middle and upper-middle classes will have no choice but to throw money and people at our crime, drug, poverty, and medical problems by supporting greater social service expenditures. However, I know from a lifetime in elected politics that it is much more likely that the middle and upper-middle classes will simply acquiesce in the construction of rural prison camps for the criminals[13] while allowing the underclass to murder one another or die of drugs, AIDS, and neglect before they cough up more money.

The glory of New Deal America was that nearly everyone identified with the unemployed working class; it was all the rest of us versus the plutocrats of Wall Street. Today, things are almost exactly reversed: the family-oriented, socially conservative middle class identifies more with the upper class than with Appalachian holler-dwellers, inner-city single parents, or armed teenage sociopaths. Charles Murray, author of the famous critique of the American welfare system *Losing Ground,* recently summarized many of my own concerns:

12. See Ellen Hopkins, "Sex Is for Adults," *New York Times,* 26 Dec. 1992, 13.
13. The unbeliever need only read recent cases all but abolishing the ancient hearsay rule (as well as the constitutional right to confront one's accusers) in rape and child sexual abuse cases in state court and drug and political corruption cases in federal court. For a detailed account of the general direction of criminal law in state and federal courts, see *State v. Rummer* (Neely, J., dissenting) 432 S.E.2d 39 (W.Va. 1993).

Let us draw together the various strands—the aging of the baby-boomers, the failure of the new wave of liberal programs, the demise of "structural unemployment," the racialization of AIDS, the unmooring of liberalism itself.

For years, the black inner city has been the symbol both of America's past failures and of its obligation to admit blacks to full equality—and it has also been an object of fear, anger, and guilt. Over the next few years, specific and quite powerful trends will effectively diminish the guilt and increase the fear and anger—especially among liberals. By the mid-1990s, what is now a more or less hidden liberal condescension toward blacks in general, and toward the black underclass in particular, will have worked its way into a new consensus.

The particular form the new liberal consensus will take depends on circumstances, but in general mainstream liberal intellectuals and policy-makers will have become comfortable believing something like this: (1) inner-city blacks are really quite different from you and me, and the rules that apply to us cannot be applied to them; (2) it is futile to seek solutions that aim at bringing them into participation in American life, because we have seen that it cannot be done; and (3) the humane course is therefore to provide generously, supplying medical care, food, housing, and other social services—much as we currently do for American Indians who live on reservations. And so we will have arrived in the brave new world of custodial democracy, in which a substantial portion of our population, neither convicted as criminal nor adjudged to be insane, will in effect be treated as wards of the state. . . . Such views would then become the baseline from which other, still more extreme measures to segregate the underclass could be contemplated.[14]

One need not agree with Charles Murray's conclusions about social matters in general to recognize that he may be like Nostradamus on this one subject. Nowhere can the prophetic nature of Mr. Murray's vision be better appreciated than in the real life drama being played out in the great progressive state of California.

In 1979 property taxes in California were more or less frozen by

14. C. Murray, "The Coming of Custodial Democracy," *Commentary* (Sept. 1988).

Proposition 13, which constitutionally prohibited a property tax that would hit the upper-middle and upper classes. In the wake of two major tax cuts at the federal level during the Reagan years, in 1991 Congress, although persisting in its refusal to raise federal taxes substantially, nonetheless mandated that states raise spending on schools, prisons, roads, and, especially, medical care for the elderly. In 1991–92 California managed to raise taxes, combining the tax hike with a great deal of belt-tightening. In 1992–93, however, taxpayers dug in their heels, so California solved its $14.3 billion crisis by simply slashing programs like education and added a proposed ballot proposition (which did not pass) to cut welfare payments by 25 percent.[15] In its middle class's willingness to let the lower classes die in the streets, California, then, is realizing the dire predictions of Charles Murray.

Proposition 13 froze California property taxes at 1 percent of purchase prices, so only utterly foolhardy older Californians will sell their houses after their children finish school and move away, unless they plan to leave California. Because property taxpayers consequently grow progressively older and richer than the parents of public school students, these property owners—now in their fifties with adult children—tend to be white and significantly more affluent than the parents of the Hispanic, Asian, and black children filling the classrooms of elementary schools and high schools. Public school enrollment in California is increasing at roughly two hundred thousand pupils a year due to immigration, yet the children involved are not the children of property taxpayers, so who cares about Proposition 13? Simply put, the costs of illegitimacy and divorce-related poverty are being paid for by school children through a very complicated shell game of shift and shaft politics.

Although all parts of the social safety net, including public hospi-

15. In fact, Proposition 13 allows the shell game of mandating services without funding to go one step further at the state level. California, under Proposition 13, has the right to reallocate the percentage of local property taxes that are to be used to support the public schools. In order to close the budget gap in 1992-93, California lowered its appropriation from the general fund but made up the difference by increasing the allocation of property tax money to the schools. This allocation directly reduced the amount of money that local governments were able to use to provide such essential services as police protection, fire protection, and road maintenance. Ultimately, cuts in local government services end up paying for the growing medicare and SSI budgets. I suspect that some state legislators thought that by cutting local services for the middle class, pressure would build to repeal Proposition 13. That seems to me to be a pipe dream.

tals, prisons, and public schools, are severely overburdened, no division of government is quite as overburdened and demoralized as the old state departments of welfare (now frequently called "the department [or division] of human services"). Welfare departments continue to pay cash grants to the poor, usually from the federal aid to families with dependent children (AFDC) and food stamp programs, but they now must also provide a variety of direct services like child protection, collection of alimony and child support, housing of the homeless, provision of shelters for run-away adolescents, and provision of residential facilities for the mentally and physically disabled. In addition, they have assumed responsibility for most of the juveniles adjudged delinquent by the courts.

Because illegitimacy, divorce, and parental neglect are increasing eligible claimants for welfare's money and services much faster than the general population, all welfare departments suffer a yearly funding crisis. And, it is not just big cities like New York and big states like California that must redirect money from other programs like highways, bridges, and police protection to welfare. Every other big city and state government is doing exactly the same thing. Even in white rural West Virginia—the virtual antithesis of New York City or California—the Department of Health and Human Services in 1990 was so close to bankruptcy that all the accumulated surplus in other departments' special revenue accounts[16] was transferred to DHHS. Far from expanding services, this infusion of cash simply allowed DHHS to pay hospitals and other providers that hadn't been paid for more than six months.

Welfare departments' constant uphill battle to meet basic constituent needs is arduous enough when welfare executives and staff share professional pride and a desire for public service. Although my own state's welfare department fortunately falls into this category, big city welfare departments are usually provider-driven, patronage-ridden, and thoroughly corrupt institutions where the cynosure of the entire operation is the award of government contracts to the administration's political friends.

16. A special revenue account comes from user fees that are dedicated to support a particular government service. When the fees generated exceed the cost of providing the service, a surplus arises that the legislature can use elsewhere, although logic would imply that the money should be used either to expand the service generating the fee or reduce future user fees.

The Department of Human Services (DHS) in the District of Columbia offers one example. DHS receives one-quarter of the District's total revenues. This translates into an $850 million annual budget and more than seven hundred separate contracts with private providers. With contracts for homeless shelters, welfare hotels, housing of the mentally retarded, nursing care for bedridden seniors, maintenance of AIDS patients, and rehabilitation of crack addicts, an incumbent Washington city administration can line the pockets of its supporters, particularly if the facilities and services actually provided are Dickensian while the fees collected are bounteous.

The 1990 federal district court trial of David Rivers, a former Washington, D.C., director of human services, and his businessman friend, John Clyburn, offers insight into the typical big city, provider-driven welfare department.[17] Although ultimately acquitted, the pair was accused of conspiring to divert millions of dollars worth of DHS contracts to firms owned by Mr. Clyburn and his associates. Wiretap and tape-recorder evidence presented at *United States v. Rivers, Clyburn* dramatizes the mentality of big city welfare departments. When David Rivers was promoted from director of DHS to secretary of the District, John Clyburn expounded on the methods of replacement that the mayor should use to fill Mr. Rivers's old post: "MB [Marion Barry] would have to be the worst politician on Earth to go in and bring somebody in from out of town to head DHS," he said. "I mean that's the whole constituency. That's the political base. . . . That's where all the favors get done." Clearly Mr. Clyburn was not talking about favors for Washington's downtrodden, but for politically active welfare providers.

David Rivers's jubilation at his promotion from director of DHS to secretary of the District prompted him to comment to FBI agent Roy Leonard Carol: "I mean I was ready. I ain't gotta worry about all of the welfare shit no more, man. You ain't got to worry about a lot of homelessness and pregnancy. Who's got AIDS . . . and all this kind of bullshit."[18]

It would be contrary to everything I have learned about politics to

17. A good summary of the case can be found in, M. Willrich, "Department of Self Services," *Washington Monthly* (Oct. 1990). The trial was also covered extensively by the *Washington Post.*

18. It is true that few people in public life can withstand total scrutiny of their private conversations. I include the quote because the volumes of other evidence presented at trial indicate that this really is a faithful summary of how David Rivers felt about his work.

believe that things are much better in other big cities where welfare contractors make campaign contributions, organize fund-raisers, and get out the vote. Supposedly the democratic process supplies a counterweight to the power of providers and welfare bureaucrats, but the political reality is that welfare consumers are either too young, too mobile, or too incompetent to vote.[19]

Although welfare costs are rising across the board in the same way that all other costs are rising, there are two components of welfare budgets that are rising meteorically, namely medicaid (the program that provides medical care to the poor) and all child-related services. (Medicaid costs are roughly two and a half times the total cost of AFDC.) Medicaid costs are driven not only by expensive advances in medical technology, but also by the increasing prevalence of health problems related to teenage pregnancy and an explosion in the number of claimants needing government health care due to divorce.

When a premature child is born to an adolescent, the child's initial hospitalization alone may cost more than $200,000, but that is simply the price of the immediate neonatal services necessary to ensure the child's survival. If the child is developmentally disabled, the likelihood of which increases exponentially with severely premature children, the department of welfare, in cooperation with the federal government, must institutionalize the child for his or her entire life, provide expensive medical care, and, under federal handicap law, provide an "appropriate" education whatever the child's condition. Each child subsequent to birth, then, costs a bundle year in and year out, with the burden being cumulative.

19. One of the things I remember from my days as a young politician in the early seventies was the fiendish delight older politicians took in giving "fatherly" advice to young, liberal candidates. The spiel I remember most vividly was "to get out and meet the voters personally, specially all those people on welfare."

Many a young idealist has trudged around impoverished city ghettos or has driven up rural hollers to chit-chat with those he or she thought were among their God-given constituency. Meanwhile, back at the courthouse, the old-timers were laughing heartily because they knew that they had every voting welfare client on the machine's election-day payroll. The local incumbent organization typically hired heads of household for $100 a worker on election day to round up five to ten friends and relatives who would faithfully vote the organization slate. Furthermore, there was never any surprise about how the welfare precincts, where people voted early and often, would turn out. The losing liberal candidates didn't understand that politics among the poor is about money and not about ideas, so they wasted valuable time talking to the people they wanted to help instead of talking to independent, middle-class voters or raising money to buy votes themselves.

The imminent collapse of our social safety net is not related entirely, or even primarily, to poor blacks. The current white illegitimacy rate of 19 percent demonstrates that it is a working-class, middle-class, and even upper-middle-class phenomenon as well.[20] But divorce is also one of America's big poverty makers, which makes it perhaps the leading cause of public bankruptcy among the blue-collar and middle classes. Two-parent families, for example, have a significantly better chance of finding private health insurance than a household headed by a divorced single parent because in a two-parent family either parent might land a job with family health benefits.[21]

The second major area of rising welfare costs is direct services for children. In the early seventies, when I first became a judge,[22] there were at most five cases a year in our state supreme court involving actions by the welfare department to terminate parental rights. Today, there are twenty to thirty such cases a year. Some of the case increase, of course, emerges from greater sensitivity to child welfare matters, but most of the case increase may be ascribed to increases in instances of serious child abuse. Most child sexual abuse occurs in households where males are surrounded by two generations of females to whom they are unrelated by blood. There is child sexual abuse between parents and their natural children, but in the overwhelming majority of cases of proven child sexual abuse in our court the abuse occurs between persons living together who have no blood tie.

The yearly increases in child neglect, child abuse, and adolescent runaways are straining foster care facilities to the breaking point. There is a big difference between a normal baby and a troubled fourteen-year-old boy when it comes to finding a family to take the child in. While most metropolitan areas have good temporary shelters for runaways and troubled children, the best facilities limit any child's stay to somewhere between thirty to sixty days, so if a child can't sort out his or her problems in a comparatively short time, it's usually a

20. Table 87, *Statistical Abstract of the United States* (1992).

21. Married women throughout America take low-paying jobs as school cooks, courthouse janitors, or clerical employees at colleges to get family health insurance, while their husbands start businesses, work in the construction trades, drive overland trucks, or find other work with good cash wages but no fringe benefits. An employee of the State of West Virginia who converted her state-paid-for family health insurance for a family of four to a private plan paid $457 a month in 1993.

22. I was then thirty-one, now I'm in my early fifties, so this isn't written from the vantage point of a complete Neanderthal.

succession of foster homes and all of the squalor and ill treatment associated with long-term care. As opportunities for women have opened up outside the home since the late seventies, the quality of foster parents (who are paid fees for their services by the welfare department) has steadily declined. Today high-quality foster parents at any price are rarities due to the decrease in care-givers at home available for duty and, correspondingly, the increase in the severity of problems that those who need care suffer.[23]

In West Virginia, I estimate that we urgently need more than five beds for every bed we currently have for disturbed adolescents.[24] Ironically, the only reason we didn't reduce the number of beds for disturbed adolescents between 1988 and 1991 is that Welfare (DHHS) managed to shift a substantial portion of the total cost of dealing with disturbed adolescents from its own budget to either federal medicaid or the state department of education. That is, of course, simply robbing Peter to pay Paul, and eventually Peter will be tapped out too, even if Peter is the money-printing, deficit-building federal government.

America was a much safer, healthier, and more prosperous country

23. My source for this is my own experience and my conversations with Harry Burgess, director of child services for the West Virginia Department of Health and Human Services. Mr. Burgess, who has been involved with providing child services for more than twenty years, told me that the overall level of pathologies among children in his care is incomparably higher than it was just twenty years ago.

24. Unlike a trial judge, I don't usually get involved directly with children in need. But recently I wanted to find help for a very good boy who came to my attention. The boy had truancy and other behavior problems related to treatable learning disabilities. But his school failure was unlikely to improve because his family setting discouraged him from being home any more than necessary. Although the boy had a home, he basically lived on the street except to sleep. I called the chief juvenile probation officer of Kanawha County, summoning all of the might and majesty inherent in being chief justice of the state and the officer's ultimate boss. Yet even with those incentives to creative efforts, the probation officer told me that there was absolutely no program outside of the public school system to help a child who needed tutoring in a supportive residential setting.

Thereupon, I suggested that the child could get a ski mask and double-barreled shotgun, walk into the Charleston National Bank, hold the place up, and then surrender. In that event, my probation officer friend said, there were lots of wonderful programs to help the boy, including sending him to specialized schools out-of-state. The irony of these things is not lost on Robert Noone, a lawyer friend who regularly represents juvenile defendants in one of our rural counties. He greets his new clients by saying, "Boy are you lucky! You have just become a ward of the juvenile court, which means that for the first time in your whole miserable disadvantaged life the State of West Virginia is going to be required to spend some money to help you!"

when the divorce rate was lower. It is not necessary that divorce be abolished; it is only necessary that divorce be reduced by roughly half its present rate.[25] This, in my estimation, is entirely within the realm of the reasonable because divorce cases (in my experience) can be divided into three broad categories. About 20 percent of the time divorce is far and away the best option. Whether the problem is a violent husband, a termagant wife, a chronic alcoholic, or a completely irresponsible spouse, there are many marriages where the innocent partner and the children will be best served by divorce.

However, another 20 percent of divorces make everyone concerned worse off. These are cases where nothing is wrong that can't be corrected with a little maturity and mutual accommodation. In these cases divorce becomes the preferred option only because one or both partners have been led to believe that in a marriage anything short of perfection must be resolved by divorce. Sometimes couples who are thoughtlessly headed for divorce are saved from folly by friends, relatives, ministers, and even lawyers. But many couples still needlessly end up divorced.

Finally, 60 percent of divorces fall between the two extremes. When the emotional relationship between husband and wife is considered alone, there is usually justification for divorce. But when the relative poverty of separate living and the effects on children and grandparents are taken into account, the balance shifts toward staying married. This, perhaps, is where the pursuit of happiness and social responsibility meet head to head. Ironically, once couples make a mature decision to stay married because other options are so dismal, the marriage usually improves because a responsible commitment on the part of both partners carries in its wake a resolve to make the best of an imperfect situation.

Although I recognize that all of this sounds like a judgmental, moralistic pronouncement, it is not intended that way. It is simply that we can't afford illegitimacy and divorce at our current rates, and they can continue to occur at our current rates only if they are paid for by school children and other users of traditional government services.

25. In 1990, 1,175,000 divorces were granted in the United States; see Table 134, *Statistical Abstract of the United States* (1992). Divorce rates are calculated as number of divorces per thousand population. In 1990, the national divorce rate was 4.7; see Table 134, *Statistical Abstract of the United States* (1992). Reducing the divorce rate would have an immediately salutary effect by reducing the number of divorces in the first year. That effect would be multiplied in subsequent years as the number of married couples would grow, while the number of divorces per year would shrink.

3

The Educational Collapse

I began writing this chapter three days after my eleven-year-old son, John, submitted his sixth grade social studies project to Sacred Heart School in Charleston. Although Sacred Heart is a private, Catholic school, it competes with the public schools in the statewide program of science and social studies fairs. Throughout West Virginia, fifth-graders do science projects while sixth-graders do social studies projects. I have done both, and I hate them equally.

About the middle of December 1991, my wife Carolyn informed me that John had to do a social studies project the following winter. I received this news with less than ardent enthusiasm. Nonetheless, young John and I began searching for an interesting topic. John has always been fascinated by medieval warfare, with its suits of armor, longbows, crossbows, and castles, so initially we thought of trying to explain why the English won the battles of the Hundred Years' War against overwhelmingly superior French forces. Ultimately, we decided that medieval military politics was too complicated for a sixth grade project.

Fortuitously, while John and I were still trying to figure out how to reduce fourteenth-century France to sixth grade terms, I was asked to testify before Congress on the liability of gun manufacturers to crime victims for crimes committed with their weapons. Although I once wrote a book about product liability law, I don't know very much about guns, so I tried to prepare myself for the congressional hearing by reading everything I could find about the great gun control debate. In the process, I discovered that the cannon had decisively changed the military balance in the world between massed hoards of nomadic hunter-gatherers and small, settled civilizations.

The Roman Empire fell, notwithstanding its well-disciplined troops and highly developed tactics, largely because by the fifth century C.E. there were just too many Goths, Vandals, and Huns to be beaten with

shield and sword technology—a problem that would not have occurred had the Romans had the cannon. The barbarians' ability to
overwhelm settled peoples endured until the end of the fourteenth
century, when Tamerlane conquered an area roughly the size of the
United States, taking up parts of what are now India, Russia, Iran, Iraq,
Syria, and Egypt. But Tamerlane was the last of the great nomadic con-
querors: the development of the firearm in the fourteenth century
made it impossible ever again for barbarians to overwhelm settled
nations. The metallurgical, chemical, and mathematical skills necessary to manufacture and use artillery were simply too complicated for
any but settled civilizations.

I thought all of this interesting and capable of being explained on
a standard poster board in about as much space as I have explained
it here, adding a few maps and illustrations. John thought that a presentation entitled "How Firearms Assured Civilization" would stimu-
late interest, so that's the project we decided to do. Then the trouble
began.

First, we went looking for books about the Gothic invasions of the
Roman Empire, the conquests of Tamerlane, and the history of firearms. The public library had nothing, the West Virginia Cultural Center library was closed on weekends (when most people would want
to use it), and the University of Charleston library had also locked its
doors for the extended Christmas break. These setbacks did not give
us an auspicious start, but we persevered, ending up in the West Virginia Supreme Court of Appeals library. The supreme court library is
connected by telephone and computer hookup to the University of
Virginia library catalog, which contains about two million titles. So
John and I began to query Charlottesville, where we discovered hundreds of useful books. Whenever we found a book we wanted, we
pushed the "print screen" button on the computer, and all the relevant
material was printed. We narrowed the field to about ten books,
which the supreme court librarian ordered from Charlottesville
through interlibrary loan. The books arrived five days later.

Carolyn insisted that we couldn't just write material, but needed
pictures, models, and illustrations as well. That's the kind of busy
work I hate. John owned a hardcover book on medieval weapons, with
color illustrations of the earliest firearms, but we did not want to cut
up the book, so we needed color photocopies. The West Virginia Supreme Court does not have a color photocopier, but another state

agency does. A trip to the bowels of the capitol caused perfect color copies to materialize miraculously.

Meanwhile, Carolyn bought papier-maché mix, paint, and little plastic soldiers from a hobby shop to make a model of Hadrian's Wall being overwhelmed by barbarians. She spent an additional twelve hours on the project supervising preparation of the bibliography, filling out the outline form provided by the county board of education, and helping John with other paperwork. I spent three hours (some of them in the car while John and I were going skiing), explaining the history of Rome and the invasions of Tamerlane and then two additional hours (divided into fifteen-minute segments) helping John rehearse his speech to the judges.

In the end, John was quite proud of his project, and he acquitted himself handsomely in his oral presentation. However, John did not win, nor did he even get honorable mention. I went down to the school the night of the social studies fair when all the projects were publicly displayed and looked at the competing entries. Most of the students had projects that, in their own ways, were just as elaborate as John's. There were projects on everything from ecology to the Salem witch trials, and, although a few were entirely modest efforts, I was amazed at how well done most of them were. Although many parents had advanced degrees, the great majority did not, and about half the projects that either won or received honorable mention came from children whose parents hadn't graduated from college.

The question, of course, is, Whose project was this? When I first got word that I was to "help" John do a social studies project, I thought the whole undertaking was *my* project, and I resented the hell out of being forced to do a lot of busy work to keep my son from looking stupid. But then I realized during John's rehearsals for his speech that he had a firm grasp of (1) what the Roman Empire was; (2) when the Romans flourished; (3) how the Huns from the central steppes of Asia set in motion other bands of barbarians like the Goths; and (4) how Tamerlane was the last nomadic conqueror because of advances in artillery. It was then that I realized that this whole exercise was also John's project.

In the course of doing this apparently stupid project John had learned how computers and telephone lines link distant databases, how a university catalogs its books, and how a person goes about doing library research. But it was Carolyn and I—the parents—who taught

John these things, and not his teachers. Indeed, parents from all walks of life had successfully participated in this drill, bringing to their children's educations their own pertinent knowledge and experience.

In West Virginia, the science and social studies fairs mobilize everyone. While I was helping John with his project on firearms, a full-time homemaker called me from out of the blue and asked if I would be willing to be interviewed by her daughter for a high school social studies fair project on crime. I readily agreed and devoted an hour and a half to a tape-recorded interview about prisons, prosecutors, and courts. The mother who asked for the interview is a high school graduate who was putting in at least a forty-hour workweek to make her daughter a successful competitor.

After I realized how much a child could learn in our library, I invited all the sixth-graders in the "gifted" program at Marmet Elementary School—the West Virginia Supreme Court's partner school—and showed them how to research their social studies projects through the telephone/computer data link. Doing this with the children at Marmet has now become a yearly event for me and my law clerks. Other daddies, mommies, and the companies they work for do even more spectacular things in the science fair. Supervisors and plant security turn blind eyes every winter as pipes, test tubes, copper wire, batteries, glass tubing, flasks, basic laboratory chemicals, telephonic equipment, and electronic gear head home either permanently or on loan for the construction of electrolysis apparatuses, distillation devices, electromagnetic displays, and chemical magic.

In grade school and high school projects like West Virginia's science and social studies fairs, the middle class has an enormous advantage. Isadore Adler, a great science professor from the University of Maryland, once told me how, when he was judging biology exhibits in a Baltimore citywide high school science fair, he discovered an extraordinarily talented two-boy team from a truly dismal inner-city school. When he asked the boys to explain the most difficult "methodological problem" that they had had to overcome, they replied, "Getting the equipment!" Educated middle-class parents who can find equipment can give their children a decisive edge in city, county, and state competitions. More important, such parents can and do give their children the edge in more important competitions—namely, the SAT exam that leads to Merit Scholarships. Parents who expect success from their children, and are willing to see to it that children get the support necessary to be successful, generally have successful children. Going through school, for those who don't remember, is both damn difficult and no fun.

I was an extremely poor student through the fourth grade and a decidedly mediocre student through the eighth grade. I did not read with any competence until the sixth grade, my handwriting is miserable even today, and I was never an accurate mathematician. I know a few people who breezed through good schools on their native smarts, but I don't know very many. Even for people like me who had supportive, ambitious parents and enough money to attend the best schools in the world, going through school was real, real tough. In short, it is no piece of cake to get our children educated in the best of circumstances.

The consistently poor performance of American grade school, middle school, and high school students compared with the same students from European and Pacific Rim countries demonstrates that we are doing something very wrong in the schooling process between the first and twelfth grades. Viewing such objective criteria as funding levels, construction budgets, and teacher competency, it is difficult to conclude that whatever we are doing wrong involves either a lack of commitment to education or an unwillingness to pay for superior quality.

The top end of American education—college and graduate school education—is the best in world. Our problem lies in educating children rather than adults, and that fact alone implies that our problems in primary and secondary education are fundamentally a function of the students. The quality of our schools compared to the schools of other countries is roughly the same at all levels, but as soon as the American system is given motivated students (i.e., adults who want to be in class), America's performance skyrockets to stellar heights, leaving every other system in the world far behind.

Our problems with regard to the bottom half of our labor force, the preeminent victims of America's poor primary and secondary education, are best illustrated by Figure 2.[1] According to the 1986 National Assessment of Educational Progress, only four in a thousand thirteen-year-olds and sixty-four in a thousand seventeen-year-olds could correctly answer this question, which is appropriate for eighth grade stu-

1. Answer: 30

Figure 2.

R?	S	40
35	25	15
T	V	W

R, S, T, V, and W represent numbers. The figure is called a magic square because adding the numbers in any row or column or diagonal results in the same sum.

What is the value of R?   __ 30   __40   __50   __Can't tell

dents. This poor performance is frightening for economic if not for social reasons. Our competitors in Europe and the Pacific Rim are steadily gaining on us in the competition for plants because they are producing skilled production workers who have twelve years of strong, formal schooling. Thus in Europe and industrialized Asia, students who are not college-bound would be able to answer this question in large numbers by the time they are seventeen. These superior production workers are then able to learn new skills on the job or in short-term training courses more quickly and thoroughly than American workers.

The dismal success rate of American children with regard to the magic square should not surprise us if we look back to our own childhoods and the effort it took us to learn to read, write, calculate, and spell. The first six grades of school are not only hard, but they are also supremely boring. Learning to read, write, calculate, and spell requires drill, drill, drill, and more drill. Good teachers try to make this drill as much fun as possible, but nobody ever disguised school's tedious nature for me. Until the seventh grade (when school finally began to deal with ideas) I hated school as much as Huckleberry Finn did. Furthermore, my father hated school, my wife hated school, and now my son hates school. Indeed, among my friends it is hard to find someone who did not hate at least the "school" part of school, even if he or she enjoyed going to school for the social distraction.

School doesn't work very well without homework, yet children uniformly hate homework, and even geniuses like Albert Einstein and Winston Churchill wouldn't do homework without coercion. Most of the time, children can't do their homework alone because there is something (or everything) that they don't understand. This is particularly true when reading skills have not developed to the point where children can understand written directions. Consequently, parents must supervise homework, which in most cases means actually doing the homework with (if not for) the child. As educators are now coming to appreciate, however, homework can be the most divisive element in family life, and it places great stress on both parents and children. Overworked, indifferent, or self-absorbed parents can't cope with the stress inherent in coaxing and coercing children to do homework, so grade schools, middle schools, and high schools aren't nearly as successful as the money we pour into them would seem to warrant. Colleges and graduate schools, in contrast, are overwhelmingly successful because parental supervision is no longer the cynosure of student success.

When I was a boy in the early 1950s I had a few friends whose parents would beat them if they didn't earn high grades. As I remember, this had no effect whatsoever on the children's study habits; they simply got beaten after every report card, which made school a supremely negative experience. Yet the beating technique has the charm of removing the parent from the arduous process by which good grades are earned. In immigrant families and others where parents *can't* help with homework, the beating technique is at least understandable insofar as illiterate, mystified, or mathematically naive parents can say only, "Do your homework, study hard, do whatever is necessary to get A's—or else!"

This brings us to the prime fact of education that everyone ardently wishes to deny: Primary and secondary education depends about 60 percent on students and parents and only about 40 percent on teachers and schools. Of course, when highly motivated students are combined with superior teachers, as they are in the great upper-middle-class public schools (e.g., those in Bethesda, Maryland, and Larchmont, New York), or in the great St. Grottlesex private boarding schools, the results are spectacular. The spectacular results, however, are because of the students, not because of the teachers. Groton and St. Paul's seldom accept candidates below the fiftieth percentile on the secondary school scholastic aptitude test (SSAT), which populates their schools with students having an ability rating well above the ninety-fifth percentile compared to all children that age in the United States.[2]

2. SSAT exam-takers are usually children from ambitious, middle-class families. In addition, institutions that search for talent, Johns Hopkins University, for example, pay

In high school I worked one hour a day for half a year memorizing irregular French verbs and, to this day, I can remember the imperfect subjunctive of verbs like *boire, devoir,* and *venir.* When I was at Dartmouth, I taught French in the language lab, and although I could help students with their accents, I could not help them with irregular verbs. No teacher can teach a foreign language's irregular verbs; no teacher can teach the scientific vocabulary of biology; and no teacher can teach the valences of the elements in the periodic table. All of these things must be memorized by the student, and the only way to do that is straight-up, brute-force work. An inspiring teacher may be able to motivate a student to want to apply the brute force, but the student must do all the work.

This leads me to the stories that we tell one another about education. A mainstay of the support for public education in America ironically comes from people who have themselves received only a modicum of education. I know many parents who quit school themselves at sixteen because they just couldn't stand anything about formal education who would be appalled if their children told them that they didn't want to go to college. In many unexpected places, like West Virginia, education is the last sacred cow of state and local government. With a per capita income forty-ninth in America, West Virginia ranks twenty-third in per capita expenditures for education, which means that there is a lower level of overall cynicism about the value of education in my home state than about any other government function. Traditionally, working-class people have looked to education as the preeminent tool for their children's upward mobility.

In the public debate about schools, the emphasis is constantly on the need for better teachers, less administration, and better facilities. Seldom do we hear anyone point out that what we really need is better students. Give me the building and faculty of the most miserable New York inner-city public school or the most wretched rural Appalachian school, but let me put St. Paul's student body in either one, and I'll show you a school that will go off the charts on every standard test.

---

the $55 test fee for students who are targeted as gifted by their local schools and who can't pay the fee themselves. This means that the sample of children who take the SSAT test at each grade level is much better prepared than the total universe of American children in each grade.

St. Paul's student body just wouldn't allow bad teachers to get in their way; they would study the textbooks, suck up what they could from the few faculty who weren't simpletons, and educate one another from their own reading. It is peers and not teachers that America's upper classes are buying for their $20,000 a year in tuition, room, and board when they send their kiddies off to good New England prep schools. Students learn most from their peers, so the smarter, more ambitious, harder working, and better educated the other students in any school are, the more everyone flourishes.

In the 1950s I went to a private school that had moved from Europe to the United States to escape the Nazis. The school was located on the old Winthrop estate in Lenox, Massachusetts, very close to the Boston Symphony Orchestra's Tanglewood property. Old Man Winthrop had loved exotic birds, so he had built a large structure in which to house his bird collection. The ceiling of this structure was higher than the ceiling of a traditional chicken coop but lower than the ceiling of a house, and about every ten feet there was a little round door about fifteen inches high so the birds could go in and out. My school had converted this bird palace into what we called the "class house"—the building where our classes were held. The class house had a primitive heating system, but when the temperature went below zero, we all needed to wear our jackets inside, and steam emerged all winter from the teachers' mouths as they lectured.

Although the Lenox public library was extraordinarily good, my school's library was a disaster, and the dormitories would never have passed inspection if the place had been a state-operated school for juvenile delinquents. Although the campus was beautiful and the food better than average, the place was otherwise a dump. Nonetheless, the teachers knew their subjects and were surpassingly enthusiastic, so the school radiated with excitement for the arts, music, literature, politics, and even science. Not every student was willing to devote an hour a day to studying irregular French verbs, but enough students studied hard that peer pressure worked generally in a positive direction. The top half of my small graduating class had college board scores well over 1,200, and it was a rare student who had scores under 1,000. Yet the facilities of this school would be officially condemned today in any public school district.

None of this is to deny the validity of the ancient English adage that first men create buildings and then buildings create men. Yale has begotten dedicated alumni for a century with its beautiful courtyards, comfortable leather furniture, cozy library rooms, superb architecture, and beautiful landscaping. St. Paul's School in Concord, New Hampshire, has the most spectacular campus of any secondary school in the world, and most of the other St. Grottlesex schools are not too far behind. Good facilities do make life nicer, but I would rather send John, or his six-year-old brother Charles, to the Buxton School in Williamstown, Massachusetts—a bigger dump than even my old prep school—than I would to the very newest, most modern, most up-to-date school ever constructed if the students in the beautiful school weren't as good as the students at Buxton. Indeed, Buxton is one of the schools I am seriously considering for my children.

Good students perform two functions. They make it possible for the teachers to be enthusiastic, and they inspire their classmates. The single most important element in a person's education is expectations; when a person is expected by his or her parents, teachers, and peers to do well, the person usually does well. When parents and peers demand high levels of performance, most students perform well. When parents and peers expect bad performance, most students perform badly. In my opinion, the years from 1966 to 1974 were the nadir of modern American university education because students justified not working through a host of political arguments about the evils of the establishment, which then became an integral part of the peer pressure structure.

Most parents understand the power of peer pressure, but only a minority understand the relationship between parental nurture and peer pressure. In general it is not true that children identify with their peers more than with their parents. When parents are actively involved in their children's lives and behave reasonably, children identify primarily with their parents. Thus, almost all children adopt both their parents' religion and their parents' political party affiliation. This is not to say that there isn't a constant battle for a child's soul between concerned parents and peers; it is only to say that, most of the time, concerned parents win handily.

Twice a year in West Virginia we have judicial meetings where I have a chance to hear the experiences of judges from the suburbs of Washington, D.C. (Charles Town, West Virginia), the suburbs of Pittsburgh (Wheeling), small midwestern cities (Parkersburg and Huntington), and rural counties bigger geographically than New York City and yet with only five thousand people. The judges whom

I query universally tell me that in the families where the parents are concerned, the children only rarely end up in juvenile court. As one smart trial judge explained, children must be interested in something—it doesn't matter what that something is. A good high school athelete, even if he or she has below-normal intelligence and comes from an abjectly poor family, has a much lower likelihood of getting into serious trouble than a child who has no interest in anything. Computer hackers, student government junkies, cheerleaders, ballet dancers, painters, and actors all do as well staying out of trouble as athletes, but the children who pass their out-of-school hours hanging around the game room at the mall or cruising with their friends are headed for problems.

Occasionally a child prodigy teaches himself or herself to play a musical instrument or sets out to read all of Gibbon's *Decline and Fall of the Roman Empire* before the age of twelve in spite of negligent or indifferent parents, but such children are rare. Certainly neither I nor any of my friends has ever met one. Children get interested in school work, hobbies, or sports because someone—usually one of their parents—encourages them in these pursuits. I tried to introduce John to music only to discover that all music is noise to him. And, no matter what I do, I cannot get John interested in experimenting with a computer. John will use a computer to write his school papers, but he is not interested in a computer as a scientific toy. I introduced John to skiing when he was six, and for the first three weekends he became frustrated, got cold, fell down, and cried a lot. The next year, however, he began to enjoy skiing, and now skiing is his favorite pastime. John loves to shoot skeet, although all gun sports bore me to tears. John is an indifferent horseman, although I've loved riding all my life. John can camp in the woods for weeks at a time, while anything vaguely touching the outdoors feels like Vietnam to me.

In short, getting children interested in something is not nearly as easy as it seems. Some children take naturally to their parents' interests, others do not. What usually happens is that a child takes naturally to some of the parents' interests but not to others. When a child rejects what interests his or her parents, the parents must stretch themselves to find constructive pursuits the child will enjoy. The whole process requires lots and lots of work. If the only thing the parents find interesting is hanging around the game room at the mall or cruising, then the children go down the tubes.

Seventy-five years ago, when a quarter of the American population was still farmers, it was easy to find something useful for children to do. Even in cities, children typically found part-time work at the age of thirteen and quit school at sixteen. When I was a boy, people still boasted that they were high school graduates. But now those easy and natural ways of keeping children out of trouble (although still prevalent in less developed countries) are unavailable to us. Fewer than 2 percent of Americans are farmers, the teenage unemployment rate is usually more than 40 percent, and children who do not obtain training of some sort after high school are doomed to the bottom quarter of the labor force.

By 1962, sociologists like Patricia Cayo Sexton of New York University were pointing out that the most prominent correlation between a child's success in life and other factors is between success in life and the social class of the child's parents.[3] Social class continues to be a more accurate predictor of success than intelligence, physical strength, appearance, or any other readily measurable factor. The reason for this remarkably strong and persistent correlation takes us back to the notion of "expectations." People usually aspire to accomplish what is expected of them. It is expectations that explain why some armies—like the Romans, Germans, and British—advance and die in such nightmarish battles as Arausio or the Somme, whereas other armies—like the South Vietnamese or Iraqis—beat hasty retreats at the first sound of shots fired in anger.

If a child comes from a family where parents and grandparents have been doctors and lawyers, it is likely that the child will aspire to be a doctor or a lawyer. Black educators have found that perhaps the most insidious racism—low expectations for black students—is pervasive at all levels in American society. At the simplest level, a total stranger is more likely to inquire about athletics or music instead of academics when talking with a black child than with a white child. In a stereotypical sort of way, black children are expected to excel in athletics and music, whereas white children are expected to excel in computers and pre-med.

The leading article on the effects of low expectations on minority children was written by Claude M. Steele, a black sociologist at Stanford.[4] According to Professor Steele, more than half of black college

3. See Patricia Cayo Sexton, *Education and Income* (New York: Viking Press, 1961).
4. Claude M. Steele, "Race and the Schooling of Black Americans," *The Atlantic* (April 1992).

students fail to complete their degree work for reasons that have little to do with innate ability or environmental conditioning. The problem, he points out, is that black students, from the outset of their school days, are undervalued in both malevolent, racist ways and subtle, unconscious ways. The latter type of deprecation is all the more insidious because it is engaged in by sincere friends, thus making low expectations all the more credible. Most pertinent for my argument, Claude Steele argues:

> Despite their socioeconomic disadvantages as a group, blacks begin school with test scores that are fairly close to the test scores of whites their age. The longer they stay in school, however, the more they fall behind; for example, by the sixth grade blacks in many school districts are two full grade levels behind whites in achievement. This pattern holds true in the middle class nearly as much as in the lower class. The record does not improve in high school. In 1980, for example, 25,500 minority students, largely black and Hispanic, entered high school in Chicago. Four years later only 9,500 graduated, and of those only 2,000 could read at grade level. The situation in other cities is comparable.[5]

Professor Steele is focusing on blacks, but his analysis of the effects of expectations on students is just as true for whites. Increasingly, America is setting up a two-tiered educational system. The first tier is comprised of hard-working, largely middle-class students competing for scholarship money and places in elite colleges and professional schools. Students in the second tier typically do little work, learn next to nothing, yet find it surpassingly easy to sail through school, get a high school diploma, and then, should they suddenly become motivated to work, enter a state college or university, where the only entrance requirements are often a worthless diploma and a beating pulse.

The only thing that can be said for the way we manage the second tier is that it is to our credit, in stark contrast to Europe or Japan, that we offer a limitless number of second chances to any student who wants another try. We do this through the unheard-of and terribly expensive vehicle of offering remedial math and remedial reading at the

5. Steele, "Race and the Schooling of Black Americans," 68.

college level. Our system's major problem is not that it fails to demand high entrance requirements the way the Europeans and Japanese do when students go from basic education to high school and from high school to college, but rather that so few students in the second tier who have blown off grade school and high school because of inadequate parental nurture are motivated to grab the second chances we offer. Here expectations, confidence, and money all play a role.

The first tier of competitive students are motivated by parents, peers, and the schools their parents have carefully selected for them through paying tuition or living in high-tax, high-cost-of-living school districts. Even before the first grade, the first-tier students are expected to excel (I know a public school with homework in kindergarten) and, from my observation, first-tier students are working much harder than their counterparts did a generation ago. Although first-tier students suffer stress beginning in the third or fourth grades as a natural result of parental and peer pressure, they nonetheless are sustaining America's competitive position in world markets.[6]

Overwhelmingly, children on the competitive track have ambitious, supportive parents. If a person sits very long as a judge, he or she reads hundreds of presentence reports from probation staff about convicted criminals. My colleagues in the trial courts assure me that the one attribute common to all juvenile delinquents is a lack of "connectedness" to the major institutions of society—churches, synagogues, Boy Scouts, Little League, school athletics, and part-time employment. Being connected for a child involves lots of work for a parent. Children go to activities; activities do not come to children. When parents are overworked, ignorant of parenting skills, or self-absorbed, children can't even get to the compensatory programs that we have put in place for the express purpose of making up for overworked, ignorant, self-absorbed parents.

If the reader is tempted to disbelieve my unpleasant conclusions, a comparison of America to our seeming economic nemesis Japan will cinch the matter. It is fashionable these days to bemoan superior performance of Japanese students compared with their American coun-

---

6. It is from the pool of top students that I always select my law clerks. Students emerge from this demanding process with enormous depth of background, and I need my clerks to teach me. I seldom ask how a clerk applicant did in law school; I ask how a clerk applicant did in high school and college, and I ask in great detail about a clerk applicant's language, math, and science background.

terparts. Indeed, on standard tests of mathematical skills the United States ranks well below Japan, Korea, Taiwan, and most of Western Europe.[7] Yet, the superior performance of students outside the United States is entirely unrelated to superior education systems, at least if education systems are measured by such objective criteria as teacher credentials, teacher to student ratios, absolute expenditures per student, or education expenditures as percentages of Gross National Product.[8] Table 1 compares Japanese and American education.[9] West-

Table 1. Comparison of Educational Resources by Country

	Schools	Teachers	Students	Students per Teacher
Japanese Education				
Primary	24,852	445,000	9,607,000	22
Secondary	16,774	570,000	11,265,000	20
Third-level	1,145	145,000	2,581,000	18
GNP for education = 5.0 percent				
Literacy rate = 99 percent				
U.S. Education				
Primary	71,608	1,306,001	25,506,170	20
Secondary	29,442	977,079	14,786,138	15
Third-level	3,406	772,000	7,117,000	10
GNP for education = 6.7 percent				
Literacy rate = 97 percent				

Source: *P.C. Globe, Inc.,* Tempe, Ariz. (1992).

7. See A. E. Lapointe, N. A. Mead, and G. W. Phillips, *A World of Differences: An International Assessment of Mathematics and Science* (Princeton: Educational Testing Service, 1989), and L. Comber and J. Keeves, *Science Achievement in Nineteen Countries* (New York: John Wiley, 1973).

8. Japan has the highest elementary and secondary school science and mathematics test scores in the world. However, Japan ranks below the United States, Canada, France, Netherlands, and Belgium in student to teacher ratios, quality of teachers, facilities, and class size. See M. Howarth, *Britain's Educational Reform: A Comparison with Japan* (New York: Nissan Institute-Routledge, 1991).

9. The objection can be raised that Japan's superior performance, compared with that of the United States, has to do with our shorter school year. I don't believe there is much correlation, but even if a longer school year explained Japan's superiority over the United States, it would not explain Japan's superiority over Western Europe, where the school year is about as long as in Japan.

ern European countries that out-perform the United States spend slightly more per pupil than Japan, whereas Pacific Rim countries like Korea and Taiwan spend substantially less than Japan. Japanese students, however, out-perform everyone on standard tests, which is why I have chosen to compare us to the Japanese.

The Japanese spend 25.4 percent less money as a proportion of their GNP on education than we do; they have a substantially higher student to teacher ratio than we have; and they send only 23 percent of their secondary students on to third-level education, compared to our 48 percent. Japanese primary school teachers, on average, have several years less formal education than American primary teachers; Japanese school buildings do not compare favorably with American school buildings; and many schools and classrooms in Japan are substantially more overcrowded than average class size would indicate. In the United States, in contrast, student to teacher ratios are set by law and enforced by teacher unions through the courts, a situation that would never exist in Japan.[10]

No one denies that the Japanese are doing a much better job of educating children between the ages of four and eighteen than we are. There is, however, no one who denies that college and university education in the United States is the best in the world and that the Japanese send many of their college and graduate students here to be educated. In fact, the entire globe sends graduate students to the United States to be educated. If, then, we have the most expensive education system in the world, yet have substantially less to show for it at the elementary and high school levels than education systems that spend much less money, then we are not simply "screwing up" and "wast-

10. Contrary to popular belief, Japan is not the powerhouse of efficiency that it is often believed to be. The Japanese have created a powerhouse in automobiles, semiconductors, and consumer electronics, and they have exported those products around the world. But they do not encourage competition in the rest of their economy, so the rest of the Japanese economy has languished and falls far behind its American counterparts. Indeed, American productivity is significantly higher than Japanese productivity. In 1990 each full-time U.S. worker produced $49,600 in goods and services, compared to $38,200 for Japanese workers. Japanese productivity in such protected areas as general retailing was only 44 percent of that of U.S. workers. Japanese factory workers overall produced only about 80 percent as much as Americans on an hourly basis. Consequently, the Japanese are not the supermen and superwomen that the press often portrays, and, contrary to popular belief, the Japanese do not have anywhere close to the most efficient way of doing business in the world—we do. See McKinsey Global Institute, *Service Sector Productivity* (Washington, D.C.: McKinsey and Co., Inc., 1992).

ing" resources. We are doing something wrong outside the schools. The correlation that counts (at least after some basic level of facility, teacher, and textbook resources has been met), then, is not between quality education and money, but rather between quality education and something else. The "something else," most observers have reluctantly concluded, is the female labor force participation rate. Japan has the lowest female labor force participation rate in the industrial world. Typically, Japanese women work before marriage but then withdraw from the labor force during the time that their children remain at home and in school.

The typical Japanese mother, known affectionately as the "educational mom" (*koyiku mama*), is not a demanding, single-minded tutor. Rather, she has intense dedication to her children's education. Japanese mothers assist their children in doing homework if they are able; they seek to promote their children's interest and involvement in school; and they strive to create a home environment that is comfortable and conducive to study. Research conclusively shows that Japanese children do not suffer more severely than children elsewhere from school-related pressure. In one large study, fewer than 3 percent of Japanese grade school children made negative comments about their school, compared to 11 percent of American children.[11]

Comparisons with Japan inevitably elicit the observation that Japan is not a particularly pleasant place in which to live. I would not want to live in Japan, but that doesn't mean that the positive correlation between low female labor force participation and high test scores is not impressive. When mothers are home to encourage, supervise, and help with homework, more homework gets done. Because homework is the cynosure of successful learning, test scores skyrocket. What we do with an understanding of the relationship between stay-at-home mothers and test scores is up to us, but knowledge is knowledge—it is only the fool who "denies" obvious truths (like the Earth's being round) simply because recognizing a truth is uncomfortable.[12]

11. See H. W. Stevenson, "Japanese Elementary School Education," *Elementary School Journal* 92 (Sept. 1991): 116.

12. I am not being intentionally tactless by referring constantly to the "female labor force participation rate" instead of something more gender-neutral, like the "parental labor force participation rate." In the United States the average woman who works full time earns only about 65 percent of what the average man who works full time earns, and this figure does not change much from decade to decade. See Tables 710 and 713, *Statistical Abstract of the United States* (1992), and *Historical Statistics of the United*

A few years ago my editor at the Free Press was Grant Ujifusa, who is a nisei Japanese from Wyoming, wears cowboy boots, and went to Harvard. According to Grant, one of his sister's friends is a middle-aged woman who had first come to the United States about fifteen years earlier with her husband, a prominent young Japanese executive. Living immediately outside New York City, the Japanese woman observed Anglo friends being abandoned by their husbands (who typically ran off with younger women), Anglo children sent off to third-rate boarding schools because dual-career parents didn't have time to care for them at home, and Anglo women abandoning both husbands and children to run off with lovers. Commenting to Grant's sister on what she had been seeing, the woman asked rhetorically, "What are these people, animals?" If the Japanese look like conformist ants to us, we look like libido-driven pigs to them.

The difference between Japanese and American societies, of course, has a great deal less to do with moral vision than with what each society can afford. And this brings me to my observation at the beginning of chapter 1: The United States was the first country to be rich enough to make the pursuit of happiness a working-class reality. In Japan, in contrast, there is little breathing room for the pursuit of happiness. When 125 million people live together on a barren set of islands only slightly larger than California, there is little choice but to enjoin public-spirited behavior although harsh discipline. Money simply cannot be squandered by allowing people to experiment with novel or exotic family arrangements when those experiments will cause poverty for others.

Indeed, any poor country that hopes to develop must discipline its citizens to public-spirited behavior, particularly in the areas of child care, marriage, and divorce. From a purely financial perspective, when a married couple breaks up and moves to separate resi-

---

States: Colonial Times to 1970 (1975). Although there is no denying a lingering discrimination against women in the work place, the failure of the average income disparity between men and women to narrow significantly, as it has for blacks and Hispanics in comparison to whites, leads ineluctably to the conclusion that women are making many voluntary decisions that trade low stress, flexibility, and regular hours for money. Obviously, this is being done in large part so that domestic duties can be better integrated with outside work. Therefore, as long as the large disparity between male and female earnings continues, it is only reasonable to talk about the female labor force participation rate because if one parent is going to give up money to care for children, it will inevitably be the parent who earns the least money.

dences, it is impossible for them to duplicate the quality of life they enjoyed while living together because of the destruction of economies of scale. For Japan, a country on the brink of starvation a bare forty years ago, divorce would not be a custom much in vogue. Stable marriage to one partner for life is economically advantageous for society as a whole, regardless of its emotional disadvantages for the parties. Appearances to the contrary, Japan is not truly rich by American standards even now. Certainly such prosperity as exists in Japan has not been around long enough to have changed centuries-old cultural patterns.

Although Japan's GNP has grown by leaps and bounds since the 1950s, wealth is still a recent phenomenon, and Japan's standard of living is not nearly what it would appear to be from the dollar value of the average Japanese wage in yen.[13] Prices in Japan are extraordinarily high; housing is cramped and expensive; and, because a high percentage of the population either needs or wants to work in Tokyo, long commutes from distant but affordable suburbs are common. Although Japanese women traditionally stay home, Japanese men work six days a week and seldom return home much before 8 at night.

The United States, in contrast, has been the richest country in the world since the middle of the eighteenth century.[14] We have always been blessed with abundant natural resources, with more than enough

13. Japan appears to be a rich country because of the dollar value of the Japanese yen. Yet it must be remembered that Japan has hardly any physical infrastructure built before 1946, which means that such things as roads are either primitive or overcrowded. Furthermore, unlike the United States, which can always fall back on its domestic agriculture, domestic oil and gas, and atomic energy, Japan is entirely dependent upon open markets in the rest of the world and upon maintaining its competitive edge in automobiles and consumer electronics. Thus, although Japan looks rich to us, the Japanese have intense anxiety about their own continued prosperity and act accordingly.

14. It is often politically convenient to disparage America's economic prowess by pointing out that America's average wage is lower than the average wage of many other countries. However, this is patent nonsense. If the average Frenchman's or German's wage is compared to the average American's wage in terms of what each can buy outside his own country, then the average Frenchman's or German's wage is higher than the average American's. But this is exclusively the result of foreign and American central bank policies that establish currency exchange rates. If we measure the average worker's wage by what he or she can buy at home, the average American's wage is far and away the highest in the world. If I take $200 five miles down the road from my house to Sam's Club (a division of Wal-Mart), I can buy more than twice as much of almost everything (with each thing being of better quality) than I can in any store in France.

land for anyone who wanted to farm, and with good natural transportation routes (long coast lines, navigable rivers, the Great Lakes, and few mountain ranges). Furthermore, during our years of rapid industrialization we had natural barriers to external invasion and little religious or ethnic strife.

Yet even in the rich United States the economies of scale for joint living are enormous, which is why children in single-parent families are America's fastest growing poor population. Utilities, for example, are cheaper when people live together. One telephone adequately serves most households, while heating, hot water, cooking, and lighting cost less per person when shared. Although most households in the United States have two cars, insurance is cheaper per car when two or more are insured together, and less gasoline is used because travel can be consolidated. It is cheaper to buy or rent one house than two apartments, and a large house or apartment is not twice as expensive as two small houses or apartments. The cost of fire and liability insurance for a couple is only about 65 percent of what it is for two people living in separate households. Family vacations are cheaper per person than individual vacations; food is cheaper per person when prepared for two or more; and one stereo, television set, washer, drier, iron, and the like usually suffices for a family of four.

These economies of scale relate to savings on direct cash outlays. There are other economies of scale that relate to quality of life and leisure, and the loss of these economies of scale have just as great an adverse impact on the educational success of children as do the loss of money. For example, most households have a well-defined division of labor. Although there is no reason that a woman cannot fix a car or a man make an outstanding beef stew, the usual division of labor is the other way around. It takes training both to fix a car and to make a stew, and at the benign level that exists in most marriages arbitrary division of labor based on sex assures specialized training in complementary skills. When couples divorce, men must cook, do laundry, care for children, shop for groceries, and perform a host of other chores that generally used to be done for them. Women, on the other hand, must maintain cars, repair plumbing, mow yards, and do other jobs that their husbands traditionally performed. Most divorced persons living alone manage to make do for themselves, but they must work much harder than married couples do at the ordinary tasks of living, and single heads of households work the hardest of all. Ironically, the United

States is rich enough that we feel comfortable sacrificing both money and nonmoney economies of scale for the pursuit of happiness, but poorer countries understand perfectly well that they cannot sacrifice economies of scale and still survive.

In 1984 my wife and I spent five weeks at Fudan University in Shanghai, where I was teaching law. In communist China, there is almost a 100 percent female labor force participation rate, and in the hundred-mile-wide belt of great urban centers that stretches along the coast from Beijing in the North to Canton in the South there is a serious birth control program that enjoins couples to have but one child.[15] Nonetheless, my wife and I were shocked by the extraordinarily traditional patterns of behavior that we found even among China's academic elite, many of whom had spent extended time abroad.

The divorce rate in China, for example, is less than 2 percent because divorce is discouraged at every turn, beginning with counselors at a person's work unit and ending with the judges in the civil courts. Although women are required to go to work, they do not appear to socialize with men outside their own families. It rankled my wife that whenever she accompanied me to a social event in the evening she was the only woman, and when faculty wives and women professors came to call on her at our quarters, only women attended. If my wife was invited out, it was to a gathering exclusively of women. And all of this sexism existed in a university whose president was a woman whose Ph.D. was in physics from MIT. Communist doctrine has always made much moment of sex equality, and there had been no shift that I could detect in the party line when I was in China, yet among the elite law students (all Communist party members) in my evening

15. In the countryside, the birth control program is much less successful than it is in the cities because the government is able to exert less control in the farm cooperatives than in the city enterprises. The farther one goes into the hinterland, the greater the extent to which centuries-old Chinese values are still dominant. Country people know that neither the government nor their farm cooperatives will take care of them in their old age. Consequently, children are the Chinese farmer's social security administration, and it is as difficult for the government to tamper successfully with that form of social security as it is for our government to tamper with our own. In the cities, on the other hand, the manufacturing, commercial, and governmental work units that provide salaries, housing, and even hot showers to their workers have credible pension programs as well as strong social and economic control over the lives of their employees. In the cities, couples with more than one child face severe work place-related sanctions, including the withdrawal of the child-care benefits provided exclusively to one-child families.

seminars, there were no women. Notably there were a few women law students and one woman law professor in my morning lectures, but the ratio of men to women was more than ten to one.

Japan and China are strikingly different societies, but their one great similarity in comparison to the United States is poverty. Their congruous social conservatism illustrates, I believe, that social experimentation is a luxury that few societies can afford, which is why the leader in life-style innovation is the United States—far and away the richest country in the world—followed closely by the wealthiest countries of Western Europe. This is not to say, however, that the successfully developing countries of Asia are not following us; it is only to say that they are following us at a great distance.[16]

My conclusions in these regards can be tested by looking at one other part of the world—the Islamic Middle East. In the Middle East, all the movement today is away from any type of poverty-generating, Western-style social innovation and toward a reaffirmation of traditional, feudal Muslim customs. Although Japan and China remain decidedly traditional, there are prominent social trends in the direction of the United States and Western Europe. In Algeria, Iran, Saudi Arabia, Syria, and Morocco, however, social initiative is in the hands of the cultural right, who are urging, and whenever possible enjoining, a return to medieval customs and values, particularly in family matters. The reason (in substance, if not in rhetoric) for this eccentric movement so at odds with the rest of the world is entirely economic. The United States and Western Europe are already very rich, Japan and China are getting richer, but the societies of the Middle East are either disappointingly stable or, more commonly, getting poorer on a per capita GNP basis every year.

All of this returns me to the notion of "externalities" that I discussed in the previous chapter. When illegitimate children are conceived, when families divorce, or when both parents become so ab-

16. Indeed, when I was in China there were recurrent campaigns against what the leadership called "ideological pollution"—the term generally used for Western influence. Students who adopted too Western a way of behaving were frequently taken out and shot in the back of the head when a particularly flagrant lapse of decorum coincided with an officially sanctioned antipollution campaign. Consequently, when reaction to what were thought to be "loose morals" came to a head, and a campaign to ferret out ideological pollution was begun in earnest, it definitely was no laughing matter. Yet the movement toward jeans, boom boxes, rock and roll, dark glasses, and Western demeanor went on and still goes on ineluctably.

sorbed by outside work that parenting functions suffer, then child-rearing costs are externalized onto the rest of society. If society is exceedingly rich by historical standards, these externalized costs can be absorbed for awhile.[17] Because the transfer of private family responsibilities to public agencies nearly always occurs at a net cost increase, however, it is politically impossible for society to absorb these costs indefinitely, partially—but only partially—because taxpayers who take care of their own children responsibly do not want to pay for other peoples' irresponsibility.

There is no better example of the effects of externalized costs than the American education system. The biggest complaint among competent teachers is that they are asked to do all the educating while parents either sit idly by or actively make the teaching process more difficult. Seventy-three percent of mothers with school-age children work outside the home. Nearly one-fourth of all children under eighteen live with a single parent. Two-parent households with only one wage-earner are truly rare; only 7 percent of all school-aged children live in such households, and these children are not spread evenly. The favored 7 percent are clustered in upper-middle-class schools and in heartland America, where lack of jobs and low cost of living make female labor force participation rates lower than the national average.

Elementary school principals think that children from single-parent homes pay a high price academically. Home life is so closely tied to school performance that 70 percent of public elementary school principals now keep formal records of each child's family arrangement. Groton's application form asks about such things as divorce, separation, and other aspects of a child's domestic background in enormous detail for the obvious purpose of weeding out those likely to be afflicted with divorce-related pathologies.

Lack of home training forces most ordinary schools to teach all of life's survival skills, something that top-notch schools have no intention of doing. According to one survey, almost all elementary schools (95 percent) teach drug education, and more than half start teaching

17. One way in which the United States absorbs these externalized costs is the same way that we absorbed externalized pollution costs in the nineteenth century—by doing nothing and letting pollution diffuse itself through nature. Much of the public cost of the externalization of child-rearing costs has come at the expense of greater crime, greater urban blight, and a general deterioration in the overall quality of life (chapter 5).

drug education in kindergarten. Most schools (72 percent) teach sex education.[18] Some rising percentage of schools, particularly inner-city schools, find it necessary to teach AIDS awareness, self-esteem, hygiene, family-life training, nutrition and fitness, environmental education, conflict resolution, and even handgun safety.

Furthermore, because no subject has been dropped from the school curriculum since the seventies, most teachers equate the calls by outsiders for more "education" in the sense of compensating courses on nonacademic subjects to pouring water into a glass that is already full. Teachers justifiably complain that they are expected to be the parent, the nurse, the policeman, the social worker, and—only at late last—the teacher.[19] When teachers are competent and indefatigable, they go a long way toward saving children who otherwise would be wrecks. But when indifferent, mediocre teachers are asked to perform these Herculean tasks, the children involved are in deep trouble.

School violence, students who haven't been read to or even talked to before kindergarten, and children who are more knowledgeable about drugs than their teachers are all problems we associate predominantly with the inner cities—that is, with poverty, minorities, and immigrants. If all of America's educational woes would fit neatly within Jesus's observation that the poor are always with us, public bankruptcy would not loom so ominously. The truth of the matter, unfortunately, is entirely to the contrary. Although the poor have more severe pathologies than the population in general, our problems in the schools extend to the children of the driven, double-income professional couples who are so self-absorbed that their children receive scant parental attention, and their children's schools receive even less parental cooperation.

The poor always have a difficult time coping. In general, the poor frequently have execrable social and parenting skills, little disposition to work hard, high incidences of mental illness, and low levels of education. Were all this not true, the poor wouldn't be the poor. The difference between now and yesteryear is that now the poor don't have any positive role models among the more affluent social classes to emulate. The poor always divorced at higher rates than anyone else; the poor always bore more illegitimate children than anyone else; and

18. "How to Teach Our Kids," *Newsweek,* special issue, Sept. 1990, 58.
19. "How to Teach Our Kids."

the poor always set up more households without the formality of marriage than anyone else. But now all these impoverishing ways of life have middle-class society's Good Housekeeping Seal. This means that the poor are becoming more and more like themselves every day. And all statistics indicate that the poor are getting poorer, sicker, and more wretched because there are no strong signals about what they should be doing.

My friend Andrew MacQueen, Charleston's chief circuit judge, tells me that there are three times as many children who are "total shits" coming into his court from rich families as there were when he took office in 1977. Judge MacQueen is an old 1960s liberal who started his career as a Legal Aid lawyer. He was elected to the bench at the age of thirty-four and is as far a cry from a conservative curmudgeon as is possible. (He even drives a motorcycle and wears a ponytail!) When asked for a more illuminating description than "total shits" of the pathologies he has observed among upper-middle-class children, Judge MacQueen began to stutter and free-associate words and sentiments like "incorrigible," "unresponsive," "selfish," "devoid of conscience," "amoral," "pathological liars," and "incapable of affection."

Upper-middle-class children who appear in circuit court are not serious criminals; they are seldom armed robbers, murderers, rapists, or arsonists. Their transgressions are typically fistfights, breaking and entering, drug dealing, and shoplifting, so they will probably not end up as lifetime prison inmates. What impresses Judge MacQueen is not these children's malevolence, but their inability to relate to others in any but the most self-centered, irresponsible way.

With two well-trained professionals raking in money like croupiers at Monte Carlo, the family incomes of our upper-middle-class delinquents in Charleston, West Virginia, are between $100,000 and $300,000 a year. Yet, the children in these families have been babysat by television and have had money thrust at them as a substitute for parental time. Instead of discipline, direction, and the self-esteem that comes from knowing that they are loved, these children have computer games, VCRs, stereos, and fancy cars. The result is that many upper-middle-class children are emotional wrecks, and their psychological problems add additional burdens to the school system.

Participation by parents of all classes in school-related activities is at an all-time low because parents simply do not have the time. It becomes more and more difficult to find parents to drive for field trips, more and more difficult to find room parents to help with holiday parties, and more and more difficult to find volunteers to organize and preside over the annual events that raise money for computers and art supplies. In the suburbs of big cities and the small towns of heartland America, much of this work still gets done, but with participation by fewer and fewer parents. The great mainstays of organized childhood recreation—Boy Scouts, Girl Scouts, Campfire Girls, Boys' Clubs, Cub Scouts, and 4-H—are in the same predicament. It becomes harder and harder to find parents to volunteer to lead these groups, particularly because the high female labor force participation rate makes it nearly impossible for most mothers to be at home in the traditional time slot for meetings, between 3 and 6 P.M.

All of this is not just important in some social sense; it is also desperately important for our economy. The competition for jobs today doesn't come from the student in the next row or the next school or the next town; it comes from children sitting in classrooms around the globe. In a world where raw materials, capital, and skilled managers can move anywhere, Americans can no longer be assured of high-wage jobs simply because they are Americans. In the current global economy, a badly trained work force not only affects the nincompoops, but it also affects bright, motivated workers who happen to be part of a work force dominated by nincompoops.

Every time schools are asked to cure problems that are better solved by parents—for example, unsafe sex, bad bicycle riding habits, careless handgun management, or inadequate conflict resolution—children are getting less of the basic drill in reading, writing, and mathematics essential if we are to compete successfully with Japan, Korea, Germany, and France. Compensatory programs take money away from computers, laboratory equipment, and teacher incentive pay, and time away from reading, writing, and arithmetic.

We will always need social programs for the bottom 20 percent of our population who have drawn life's short straws. Programs like Head Start and the Home Instruction Program for Preschool Youngsters (HIPPY) are wonderful initiatives that help disadvantaged children get ready for school. These programs are deliberate attempts to uplift the unlucky, and they are more or less free-standing undertakings that add to overall competence without subtracting from the standard school curriculum for teaching basic reading, writing, and math skills. The reason for not subtracting from the basic curriculum to insert "life skill" courses to compensate for parental neglect will become more obvious as we look at global economics in the twenty-first century (chapter 4).

4

The Economic Collapse

The miserable state of American education is troubling not because education itself is valuable. If education itself were valuable, retired people with colonnades of leisure would flock to local public colleges. The average American who is sweating over eighth grade English or college chemistry is sustained by one vision and one vision only—a steady job at good wages. The "crisis" in American education, in short, does not arise because young adults won't be able to discuss John Gay's pastoral poetry or ponder the ramifications of deconstructionist theory, but because ignoramuses can't get jobs.

We are in the process of evolving from a raw material-intensive and capital-intensive economy to a knowledge-intensive economy. Yet a large part of tomorrow's labor force is not learning to read, write, calculate, and spell in school. The young workers most in need of on-the-job training aren't seeking out that training. With all jobs that pay a "living wage" increasingly skilled jobs, this means that the United States will soon have millions of adults who cannot be employed at any acceptable family wage.

America is in trouble economically, then, not because our economy is failing to grow; not because the Japanese, Koreans, Taiwanese, and Western Europeans are besting us in world competition; and not because American overall per worker productivity no longer is the highest in the world. Rather, we are in trouble because a large and growing part of our population is suffering from severe family-related pathologies that render them incapable of availing themselves of the opportunities that the American economy offers.

In the 1960s, it was an article of faith among all economists—liberal, conservative, and radical—that a widespread expansion of jobs at good wages for five or six years would lift an entire generation of marginal workers into mainstream America. Boom times, such as existed during the two world wars, yielded jobs and the acquisition of skills to southern agricultural workers, unskilled immigrants, Appalachian hollow-dwellers, and women.[1]

Indeed, until the 1980s, there was never a time when an unemployment rate above 5 percent was combined with "good" entry-level jobs going begging. Now, however, there are jobs in every eastern American city—including such uncongested cities as Wilmington, Delaware, and Norfolk, Virginia—that pay good entry-level wages and yet cannot be filled despite an unemployment rate for young untrained workers that is regularly more than 40 percent and a nationwide unemployment rate of more than 7 percent for all workers in 1992–93.

Ogden Allied Services, one of America's largest service contractors, hires unskilled workers to perform janitorial work, to drive trucks and maintain equipment at the Wilmington DuPont plants, and to haul garbage and do plant maintenance chores for federal installations in Norfolk. In dire need of competent unskilled employees in these cities in the middle of a recession, Ogden in 1992 began negotiations with the West Virginia Department of Health and Human Services to recruit young West Virginians from our child-care facilities (schools for delinquents, foster care, and welfare department-monitored probation) for Ogden jobs in Wilmington and Norfolk. The plan was for West Virginia's DHHS to provide assisted group living for the first year until the young adults understood how to function on their own.

Significantly, Ogden was recruiting West Virginians with problems ranging from parents abusive enough that foster care was warranted to juvenile delinquency sufficiently severe to justify confinement in a residential facility (but not a reform school). According to Edward DeSantis, an Ogden vice president, these young adults (many of whom are black) would be, in comparison to Ogden's regular northeastern applicant pool, high-quality employees.

Ogden Allied Services is not McDonalds or Baskin-Robbins; Ogden provides its unskilled workers with real opportunity for advancement. The company has health insurance for employees; pays half again federal minimum wage at entry level; and guarantees punctual, courte-

1. Until the Civil Rights Act of 1964, however, blacks and women were the last hired and first fired. Even so, whenever jobs were available, women and minorities flocked to them and learned skills that, even with discrimination, made them more employable than they would otherwise have been.

ous, and reasonably conscientious employees a $10-an-hour supervisory position within a year in one of Ogden's janitorial or other unskilled operations. The motivated employee who seeks out more training and responsibility can transfer to such jobs as truck maintenance, where the hourly wage goes up to $16 and the skills learned are transferable to other companies and other geographical markets.

Of course, the Northeast corridor is notoriously expensive, so although a $10 an hour job with some fringe benefits in heartland America might afford an acceptable standard of living, such a job is less attractive in a higher cost of living area like Wilmington. In recognition of this reality, Ogden reduces working costs by providing transportation from inner-city Wilmington to the DuPont plants on the city's outskirts.[2] These benefits notwithstanding, although Ogden is usually able to fill its jobs, the turnover rate is extraordinarily high, and, according to Mr. DeSantis, few employees use work with Ogden as a stepping stone to better jobs.

Companies like Ogden usually don't get much credit or support. Detractors argue that $10 an hour is a trifling sum in the Northeast, and even that pittance kicks in only after a year of good behavior, which is a long time to wait for an impatient nineteen-year-old worker who isn't quite sure exactly what "good behavior" is. Ogden's entry-level wage of between $6.50 and $7.50 an hour translates into only about $14,560 a year before taxes. Although this wage may include health insurance for the employee as well as two weeks' vacation, a young person may reasonably prefer to hang around the street, pick up whatever money is available from the public dole, deal drugs, do odd jobs, and steal than work at an unpleasant task eight hours a day for such a pittance.[3] Others argue that the better way to get untrained

2. In addition, Ogden's personnel department will write letters of recommendation and otherwise support workers who seek to advance themselves.
3. This is not a book about welfare reform, but it would be disingenuous if I did not acknowledge that, for certain categories of people, the welfare system's design often makes not working more profitable than working. For example, if a woman is married to a man who works more than a hundred hours a month, she is ineligible for welfare, which means that she loses her medical card. The welfare rules, of course, are not designed to exacerbate human suffering, but are designed to limit exploitation and overuse of the system. Yet a family with a seriously ill child will be better off if the husband quits part-time, low-wage work so that the family can get a medical card. Then, of course, both husband and wife can look for odd jobs where they are paid illegally in cash to supplement their welfare payments and food stamps. However, similar perverse incentives do not apply to young adults without children.

young people off the street is to provide "good jobs at good wages" (by which is meant something that looks like yesteryear's GM assembly line).

Unfortunately, nothing that looks like and pays like yesteryear's GM assembly line will ever be built in the United States again. Ogden's low-wage, entry-level jobs consequently are important to the labor force of the future because taking such jobs is tantamount to going to school. The object is not to stay in a low-wage, entry-level job, but rather to learn skills (including punctuality, personal hygiene, deference to superiors, and responsibility). These skills will qualify the worker for higher-paying jobs once the worker is older, can show a track record of job performance, and has made a few contacts among higher-wage employees who will introduce the young worker to bosses and personnel officers in high-wage firms.

The two standard ways to succeed as a worker are formal education and on-the-job training. College students earn nothing for four years unless they take low-wage outside jobs. Law and medical students earn nothing for three or four years except in the summer, if they're lucky, and graduate students working as teaching or research fellows earn only a pittance. For those whose training will come on the job, the years between high school and the age of twenty-five are normally low-wage, apprenticeship years during which skills are learned and networks formed.

The great artisan unions—the plumbers, electricians, and carpenters—have formal apprenticeship programs to teach the craft to young workers.[4] Likewise, law offices, which now employ clerical employees whose skills rival those of traditional artisans, regularly take young women from high schools and career colleges for entry-level jobs. A smart and motivated woman may be promoted through the ranks of a law firm's secretaries until she qualifies as an executive secretary or legal assistant, making between $30,000 and $65,000 a year, depending on the location of the firm and the status of the partner for whom she works.[5]

4. These programs were originally designed to teach the craft to the children and relatives of union members and, notwithstanding equal opportunity employment statutes, the unions have done a pretty good job keeping most of the jobs in the family. Minorities and women have been recruited into the crafts with appropriate fanfare and congratulations, but labor's favored status among liberal politicians has resulted in much less than open admissions into the crafts.

5. Executive secretaries perform such traditional secretarial duties as composing

My own executive secretary, Debbie Atkins, is a prototypical product of the law industry apprentice program. Only in her early thirties, Debbie never attended college and yet earns more than $34,000 a year with good vacations and a superb pension and medical insurance program. As a lowly law firm clerical drudge for only slightly more than state minimum wage, straight out of high school, she decided to learn everything she could about law office computers and the practice of law. Before she came to work for me, she worked for five law firms and left all but one for a better paying job. When she started in my office, she typed opinions and other documents for my law clerks and worked only occasionally for me directly, but when my executive secretary of many years retired, she got the top job.

The difference between Debbie Atkins and the law office employees who remain clerical drudges all their lives is that Debbie is ambitious and learned how to spell, calculate, and write a clear English sentence in high school. I can teach someone as smart as Debbie how to practice law, but I can't teach someone as smart as Debbie how to read.

It was not too long ago when all American workers earned higher wages than workers abroad simply because they were Americans. As late as 1969, only 16 percent of American trade in manufactured goods was in the international sector. In 1969, few everyday products were imported because retail stores were smaller and more numerous (which increased sales and distribution costs for foreign manufacturers) and because there were few retail discount giants like Sears that could buy in carload lots from foreign producers. Foreign producers had not yet begun to manufacture the diversity of high-quality products they manufacture today. American workers consequently competed primarily with other American workers who shared the same minimum wage laws, the same union structures, and the same expectations about standards of living.

In the days when the standard of living of unskilled and semi-

---

letters, arranging their boss's schedule, making travel arrangements, receiving incoming calls, filing, entertaining visitors, and doing personal chores that range from paying their boss's bills to doing his or her shopping. Legal assistants, on the other hand, work in the professional part of law practice. They draft interrogatories, search titles, file papers in court, schedule hearings, arrange for expert witnesses, draft pleadings, and even write the first drafts of standard contracts like separation agreements in divorce cases.

skilled workers was rising, many American industries were what economists call "oligopolies." An oligopoly is an industry characterized by only a few producers–for example, steel, automobiles, and pharmaceuticals. In oligopolistic industries, cut-throat competition requiring the maintenance of low wages goes against every firm's interests. All members of oligopolistic industries dream of some scheme that will assure parallel pricing, the division of markets, and the total elimination of competition.

Under American labor laws, a union is both permitted and encouraged to organize entire industries–the Steel Workers did steel and the Auto Workers did automobiles. In an oligopolistic industry a union can ratchet up wages by exacting a uniformly high wage from every producer in the industry. In the 1950s and 1960s, oligopolistic industries like steel, automobiles, pharmaceuticals, rubber tires, and railroads simply raised prices whenever wages for unskilled and semiskilled workers increased after a strike or strike threat. Although price increases hurt sales a little, demand was so strong that both owners and workers prospered from higher prices, with consumers paying the bill.

Today, worldwide competition makes that scenario rare. Because of the multiplicity of producers worldwide, American oligopolistic industries are now competitive industries. General Motors no longer competes with just Ford and Chrysler, but now must line up against Volkswagen, BMW, Fiat, Renault, Toyota, Nissan, Yugo, and on and on. In short, it is worldwide competition that accounts for the eclipse of unions since the mid-seventies.[6] If unions raise wages the way they used to, foreign competitors will put union workers' high-wage employers out of business.

The central problem of the bottom half of the American labor force is "factor price equalization," that is to say, the free movement of capital, managers, and technology across international borders that tends to equalize the price of factors of production such as labor and capital everywhere. Labor, of course, cannot move even in the new global economy because, if it could, the United States and Western Europe would be overrun with immigrants. But labor need not be able to

---

6. In 1953, 35 percent of private-sector employees were union members. Now 16 percent of all workers are unionized, but only 11.8 percent of workers in the private sector are union members. See Fred Barnes, "Hard Labor," *The New Republic,* 22 Feb. 1993, 14.

move for factor price equalization to come into play if capital and managers can move. Factories simply will go to the workers. Determining where factories will be built involves evaluating such things as labor productivity, wage rates, taxes, regulatory and environmental expenses, and the risks of war and expropriation. As third world economies grow more stable and less risky, an American worker who cannot be more productive than a Mexican worker or an Indian worker will end up working for Mexican or Indian wages or not working at all.

During the first three quarters of this century, American workers had the advantage of being more productive than competing foreign workers because American workers were backed up by more capital. Americans invested their money in the United States because the mechanisms for investing abroad were primitive, and foreign investment was unacceptably risky. However, with third world countries now exerting themselves to appear less risky to American, European, and Japanese investors, and with sophisticated intermediaries like mutual funds, banks, and insurance companies able to move capital around the world effortlessly, American workers will have less and less of an edge exclusively as a result of per-worker levels of capital.

Capital will still be invested in high-wage countries as long as their worker productivity is commensurate with the higher wages, however. Production processes that demand complex skills will continue to be performed in high-wage countries because it is only in high-wage countries that workers with the necessary skills can be found. The migration of capital to subsistence-wage countries like India, China, and parts of Latin America will primarily transplant manufacturing processes that require nothing but strong backs and agile hands, which is why low levels of basic skills among the bottom half of our labor force is such a compelling problem.

Immediately after World War II, the United States generated more than half of the gross world product; today our share is only 22 percent. In our halcyon, post–World War II days, we were the impetus of the GATT–Bretton Woods[7] trading system, under which the United

7. GATT stands for "General Agreement on Tariffs and Trade," which is the title given to on-going trade talks (such as the Kennedy round or the Tokyo round) designed to reduce barriers to trade. Under GATT rules, every country must treat all other countries—except countries with which a country is attempting to effect a "political" union—exactly the same way. This is known as "the most favored nation principle," which sim-

States provided a market of first resort for all recovering and developing countries, particularly our erstwhile enemies and allies. Armed with the conviction that America's welfare was tied up with the welfare of everyone else in the free world, we stemmed our desire to sell our own products abroad and tolerated other countries' efforts to protect their "infant industries" even while good-naturedly opening our own markets to them.[8]

In the first twenty years of the GATT–Bretton Woods system, American imports averaged only between 3 and 5 percent of total goods and services, an insignificant figure given the sheer size of the American economy. Because our exports greatly exceeded our imports, our enormous trade surpluses purchased productive assets abroad—particularly in Europe and the Pacific Rim.

America's exports were high-technology, high-wage, high-profit products—computers and the Boeing 707 jet aircraft, for example. Because of the high level of education of American workers relative to workers in other countries, as well as the enormous amount of capital backing up every American worker, we had a virtual monopoly of the high-wage sector. Our inconsequential imports were low-wage, low-profit, labor-intensive products like children's toys and cheap shoes. The deterioration of our labor force's quality now threatens our commanding lead in high-tech, high-wage, high-profit industries.[9]

The pathologies related to family structure that prevent illiterate

---

ply means that the best deal (the lowest tariffs, the easiest access, the fewest restrictions) given to any country in the organization must be given to every country—effectively prohibiting trading blocks.

Bretton-Woods is the name of a New England resort where finance ministers and diplomats met after World War II to bang out a method of regulating national currencies in international markets. It was from the original Bretton-Woods meeting that mechanisms, like the International Monetary Fund, designed to protect currencies from violent fluctuations that would impede trade, eventually evolved.

8. I am indebted here and elsewhere in this chapter to the excellent work of Lester C. Thurow in *Head to Head* (New York: William Morrow, 1992).

9. The whole GATT-Bretton Woods global trading system was initiated, regulated, and, at times, forced upon the world by the United States, and GATT-Breton Woods was so successful that large parts of the world achieved unparalleled prosperity. Indeed, the reduction of our own share of gross world product from more than half to under a quarter in the last forty-five years does not reflect a deterioration in our own standard of living. Rather, it reflects a net increase in the standard of living of others. Furthermore, in the long run this improved standard of living for others is good for the United States as a whole, particularly if we can maintain our commanding lead in high-technology, high-wage, high-profit industries.

and semiliterate young workers from flocking to Ogden Allied Services for a leg up into the labor market also infect the competitiveness of the American labor force as a whole. If skilled workers are not available in sufficient numbers, factories can't be built, and all workers suffer as a result. Even as international trading guarantees the United States new markets, lower costs, and fast technological development, it also accelerates the rate of industrial change and makes mastery of basic literacy and numeracy skills all the more indispensable to lifetime participation in the high-wage sector. In the long run, worker productivity determines income in any country, all other things being equal—for example, the stability of the government, the integrity of the legal system, and the level of free trade in the country where a plant could be located.

American workers have prospered for centuries because all other things in foreign countries were not equal; the United States was always a more attractive place to live, work, and invest capital than other parts of the world. Now, with Europe, Japan, and the Pacific Rim meeting these "other things being equal" conditions, and Brazil, Mexico, India, and other parts of the third world nearing that point, factor price equalization will increasingly threaten the standard of living of unskilled and semiskilled American workers.

Eighty-seven percent of all goods and services[10] that Americans consumed in 1990 were produced in the United States, so productivity growth is not important just (or even primarily) for staying competitive with our international rivals. If we are to raise our standard of living in the United States, we must increase our productivity per worker so that each employed person produces more each year. This was how we raised living standards between 1947 and 1973, when average annual productivity growth in the United States was roughly 2.45 percent and median income grew at an average annual rate of 2.6 percent.

Our current dilemma, however, is that even though there has been no significant reduction in rates of investment, productivity growth

10. The service sector of any economy is extremely large and extraordinarily important. Consequently, when we talk about the goods sector of the American economy, we find a frighteningly high percentage of that sector subject to foreign competition. However, once the service sector is added to the goods sector, it becomes obvious just how much of the American economy is insulated from foreign competition and confined to Americans.

has slowed drastically. This decidedly unpleasant fact militates against fashionable "crowding out" theories that attribute our economic problems to the national debt soaking up private investment funds and wishful thinking, "lack of incentives" theories that blame excessive capital gains taxes. Productivity grew at an average annual rate of only 0.4 percent between 1973 and 1988, whereas median income rose at an average annual rate of .004 percent.[11]

The increase in the median income at a slightly faster rate than productivity growth between 1947 and 1973 derived largely from redistributive government policies. Between 1973 and 1988, the decline in skill levels of the bottom half of the labor force relative to the skill levels of the top half of the labor force slowed the rate of the increase in the median income compared to productivity growth.[12]

Democrats blame the Reagan and Bush administration policies that favored the "rich" at the expense of everyone else. Certainly the Reagan-Bush administrations did little to reduce income disparities, and rich-bashing was decidedly out of fashion, but many of the schemes that would have produced a home run for the rich, such as a reduction in the capital gains tax, never passed the Democratic Congress. In short, a reverse Robin Hood phenomenon did not occur. In constant dollars, the increase in per family income among the top 10 percent of the population in the 1980s was about a dozen times greater than the decline in per family income among the bottom 10 percent.

During the 1980s, wealth was not "redistributed" from the poor to the rich because the poor didn't have any wealth to begin with. What actually happened—politically unpleasant as the fact may be—was that the high skills of upper-income groups made them much more productive relative to low-skill, lower-income groups. World demand for highly skilled workers increased substantially during the 1980s, while the supply of highly skilled workers rose only slowly. This excess of demand over supply turned the terms of trade in favor of high-skill workers. Thus, the long years of training requisite to the professions

11. See Paul Krugman, *The Age of Diminished Expectations: U.S. Economic Policy in the 1990's* (Cambridge: MIT Press, 1990), 27. In my opinion, this slim volume is one of the best books written in the last decade for policymakers on economic issues. It is distinguished by both its clarity and incisiveness.

12. Just as progressive taxes played some role in raising median income faster than productivity growth in the 1950s and 1960s, the imposition of indirect, regressive taxes at the state level played some part in holding median income nearly constant between 1973 and 1988.

of law and medicine in the United States yielded doctors and lawyers a short-term scarcity that, at least temporarily, raised their incomes relative to others.

While worldwide demand for unskilled and semiskilled workers grew, the supply of unskilled and semiskilled workers grew much more quickly than demand, in large part because third world countries became politically more acceptable to first world capital while the technology for moving capital and managers around the world improved each year. At the same time, technology that rapidly substituted capital for labor in previously labor-intensive industries like coal mining and automobile manufacturing turned the terms of trade decisively against unskilled and semiskilled workers.[13]

Below the rarified world of business CEOs, orthopedic surgeons, and rock stars (the top one-quarter of 1 percent), the top 10 percent of American workers is populated by school administrators, industrial chemists, successful plumbers, and franchisees of two McDonalds. Mickey Kaus elucidates the fundamental shift in the nature of industry in high-wage countries that places a premium on skills, initiative, and ambition, thus leaving the bottom half of the labor force falling relatively behind:

> Suppose we gave a hundred people extensive training as actors . . . and set them loose at Sunset and Vine to seek their fortunes. What would we see if we came back ten years later? An

13. It was not simply the Reagan-era love affair with free trade that reduced middle- and working-class incomes. Incomes are even lower in the protectionist countries of the European Community, while unemployment is higher. Europe is much less hospitable to low-wage goods like textiles from Singapore and Indonesia, cheap consumer electronics from Taiwan and Hong Kong, and cars from Japan and Korea than we are. A twenty-four-inch color television set with remote control that would cost roughly $600 at an American appliance discount store like Circuit City costs roughly $2,000 in France. Throughout the European Community, ordinary J. C. Penney-quality clothing is at least 50 percent more expensive than in the United States, and even at that it is usually of somewhat poorer quality than clothing from J. C. Penney. The wonderful Casio Data Bank watch that I wear, which stores fifty telephone numbers, has an alarm, stop watch, calendar, scheduling function, and light—all for $36 at my local K-Mart—cannot be found at any price in France.

The French minimum wage for full-time workers is roughly $11,000 a year, which has resulted in a rapid rate of substitution of capital for labor. I saw such things as machines that electronically transmit credit card charges directly to the credit card company and automatic cash registers that read bar codes on packages in France long before I saw them in the United States. Yet, notwithstanding much more protectionism

equal distribution curve? Hardly. We'd see some actors working in commercials, some waiting on tables, and some, the Eddie Murphys of the world, commanding astronomical salaries. All this would make some economic sense. Eddie Murphy is worth millions, because his films make much more money than films of equally well-schooled actors who nevertheless don't have what Murphy has.

So it is in the rest of the economy, on a less dramatic scale. When the middle class consisted of workers tightening bolts on the assembly line, the difference between a superlative bolt-tightener and a merely competent bolt-tightener wasn't much, economically. As long as the bolts didn't come loose, management had no compelling reason not to pay both workers the same. But train those workers as computer repairmen, and the picture changes. The differences between a good repairman and a mediocre repairman are probably substantial, and worth rewarding. Train workers as computer *programmers,* and the picture changes even more. The difference between good and bad programmers is enormous, and employers will be tempted to recognize it with a big difference in pay.[14]

Third world governments scrambling for bolt-tightening jobs that will employ workers and generate hard currency accelerates the export of American capital and management to low-wage countries. Throughout the third world, governments are adopting pro-business policies that American managers can only dream about at home—policies like official control of labor unrest, low wages, and minimal environmental, health, and safety regulations.

The standard of living of workers is determined by a combination of productivity and the terms of trade. If A can produce three times as much as B in the same time using the same tools, A's income will be three times greater than B's income. If a particular product or service is in short supply while demand is strong, then the person with the product or service in short supply will make high profits. When the

than the United States, European unemployment was between six and ten percentage points higher than the United States (depending on country and year) during the entire decade of the 1980s.

14. Mickey Klaus, "For a New Equality," *The New Republic,* 7 May 1990, 20.

great American middle class consisted of blue-collar bolt-tighteners, America had very favorable terms of trade because most of the world was comprised of camel-drivers, sheep-herders, subsistence farmers, and Stone Age tribesmen. They all wanted manufactured goods that only the United States and Europe could produce.

There is nothing that we can do about unfavorable terms of trade, but there is something that we can do about low labor force productivity. It is productivity, far more than the terms of trade, that determines long-term living standards. The United States still has the highest standard of living in the world because we still have the highest worker productivity in the world. If the United States were considered at the top of a scale of 100 in 1992, French worker productivity was five points below at 95, West Germany third at 89, with Japan at 77, and Britain at 75 rounding out the top five.[15]

There is a general consensus that notwithstanding our high standard of living and our low level of unemployment compared with the rest of the world,[16] something is very wrong with our economy nonetheless. What bothers us is the premonition that today's young adults will be the first generation in our history to do less well than their parents. The widening gap in wages between college graduates and high school graduates among workers with five or more years' work experience augurs badly for the prospects of the bottom 60 percent of workers to outperform their parents.[17]

Indeed, the slowdown in American productivity growth since the early 1970s represents the single most important fact about our economy. Had productivity over the last twenty years grown as fast as it did for the first seventy years of this century, our living standards would now be at least 25 percent higher than they are.[18] According to Paul

15. See McKinsey Global Institute, *Service Sector Productivity* (Washington, D.C.: McKinsey and Co., 1992).

16. America's success in creating jobs stands in stark contrast to the economies that are popularly thought to be breathing down our necks. In Europe, for example, virtually no new jobs were created between 1973 and 1985. Even though Europe's labor force grew much slower than America's, unemployment during that twelve-year period increased fivefold. Japan has no better record than Europe in creating jobs. Japan has a very low female labor force participation rate, and most workers must retire from their high-paying jobs in their middle to late fifties rather than as we would, in our middle to late sixties. Thus, Japan has nothing close to full employment by American standards.

17. The ratio of earnings of college graduates to earnings of high school graduates declined from 1.5 to 1.3 during the 1970s, then rose to 1.8 during the 1980s.

18. Krugman, *The Age of Diminished Expectations.*

Krugman, an MIT economist, all of our other long-term economic concerns—foreign competition, the industrial base, lagging technology, deteriorating infrastructure, and so on—pale in comparison to the problem of slow productivity growth. All we want from the economy is a higher standard of living, so these other concerns matter only to the extent that they may have an impact on our productivity growth.

To this problem of slowed productivity growth, those running for office drone the standard solutions: greater investment in plant and equipment yielding each worker more capital, and better training for workers so that their advanced skills may eventually afford them entry into the high-wage sector of the world economy. What politicians apparently don't understand, however, is that the American economy placed about as high a share of its resources into investment in the 1970s and 1980s as in the 1950s and 1960s, and placed a much higher share of its resources into education in the 1970s and 1980s than it did in the 1950s and 1960s.[19] Thus, although productivity is influenced by both investment and public education, there is no direct, one-to-one correlation between a dollar's worth of plant or a dollar's worth of education and higher rates of productivity growth.

Unfortunately, the rate of productivity growth is probably determined by many of the same factors that determine peaks and valleys in long wave business cycles. Fifty to sixty years of relative prosperity as well as fifty to sixty years of relative recession can be the product of unpredictable and erratic changes in the rate at which technological breakthroughs are achieved.[20] In the 1950s and 1960s we were tying America together with superhighways, air transport, telephones, and computers. Other technologies, like new plastics and light-weight substitutes for steel, were reducing the cost of consumer products, while the refinement of mass marketing in chain stores like Sears and K-Mart lowered distribution costs. These dramatic break-

19. Ibid.

20. See Nikolai Kondratieff, *The Long Wave Cycle,* trans. Guy Daniels (New York: Richardson and Snyder, 1984). Between 1922 and 1928, Kondratieff published several papers dealing, in varying degrees of depth, with the question of long economic cycles. The most basic of these was an essay called "Long Economic Cycles," which was originally published in the journal *Voprosy konyunktury* (*Problems of economic conditions*) 1, no. 1 (1925). For recent commentary and modern update on the original Kondratieff thesis, see Solomos Solomou, *Phases of Economic Growth, 1850-1973: Kondratieff Waves and Kuznets Wings* (Cambridge: Cambridge University Press, 1987).

throughs facilitated the achievement of higher levels of efficiency. A superhighway connecting New York with Chicago nearly tripled a truck driver's productivity along that route; cheap telephone communications accelerated the velocity of commerce; and the Boeing 707, introduced in the early 1960s, made international business convenient and efficient.

Today, new processes and new products are constantly being developed and introduced, but the rate at which these new processes and products enhance efficiency is lower. If, however, someone invented a machine that annulled the force of gravity in a controlled way, the rate of productivity growth would immediately skyrocket beyond even the levels experienced in the 1950s.

In short, our inability to double the standard of living each generation may not be entirely attributable to low labor force skills. Yet, even acknowledging the important part that technological breakthroughs play in increasing our standard of living, productivity is also dependent on workers' skills and adaptability. If the United States remains committed to free international trade, the next fifty years will see a striking change in the nature of American manufacturing. Because a country that wants to buy from other countries must sell to other countries,[21] America's manufacturing base will maintain its position as the single most important part of the American economy, and that base will increasingly become a high-technology base.

Unfortunately, our manufacturing work force now stands at the all-time modern low of 17.6 percent and is likely to decline rather than rise as a percentage of the total labor force. Notably, reduction in overall manufacturing work force occurred simultaneously with the resurgence of American manufacturing and a striking increase in the volume of American exports.[22] This whole process is perhaps best

21. America's persistent yearly trade deficits seem to imply that foreigners will continue to sell us their goods without demanding any of our goods in return. In reality, we are selling a very valuable good to foreigners—political stability. With our enormous economy and competent but relatively conservative political institutions, the United States is a glorified safety deposit box.

22. In the early 1980s, the American economy appeared sick because of an artificially high American dollar. Much of our industry was competitive, but our currency was not. In 1985, however, we began a multiyear decline in U.S. currency so steep that only the most technologically advanced foreign countries with the lowest wages could compete with us. The only disadvantage of America's currency devaluation was that it undervalued American assets, which led, in turn, to the gobbling up of American real estate by the British and Japanese. This gave the misleading impression that somehow the Ameri-

Figure 3. Evolution of Industrial Structure

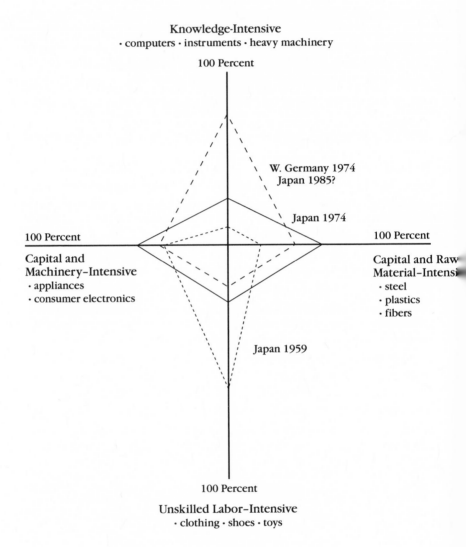

Knowledge-Intensive
· computers · instruments · heavy machinery

100 Percent

W. Germany 1974
Japan 1985?

Japan 1974

100 Percent

100 Percent

Capital and
Machinery-Intensive
· appliances
· consumer electronics

Capital and Raw
Material-Intensi
· steel
· plastics
· fibers

Japan 1959

100 Percent

Unskilled Labor-Intensive
· clothing · shoes · toys

Source: Ira Magaziner and Robert Reich, *Minding America's Business* (New York: Harcourt, Brace, Jovanovich, 1982), 80.

explained by Figure 3, which was prepared by the Japanese Economic Planning Ministry and depicts the natural evolution of manufacturing in industrial countries under conditions of free trade.[23]

As the figure shows, there is a natural evolution from labor- and
raw-materials-intensive industries to capital-intensive industries. Capital-intensive industries then evolve into knowledge-intensive industries. Knowledge-intensive industries pay the highest wages because
(so far) knowledge-intensive industries enjoy the most favorable terms
of trade as a result of natural barriers to entry. To enter knowledge-
intensive industry, a country must provide a high public investment
in education, find capital to build expensive plants and equipment,
and produce workers either experienced in or adaptable to the knowledge-intensive sector. New countries yearning to enter the knowledge-
intensive sector can't do so without government subsidies because
existing manufacturers already have dominant market shares that give
them both cost and quality advantages.[24]

Knowledge-intensive "industry" does not involve just manufacturing. In 1992, the United States had a $59 billion trade surplus in the
export of services—a fivefold increase from 1986. World-class suppliers of services include not only brand-name giants such as American
Express Co., McDonald's Corp., and Walt Disney Co., but also thousands of smaller firms like Monitor Co., a management consulting firm
in Cambridge, Massachusetts, that gets half its $60 million annual rev-
enue from abroad. Information is as much a product as an automobile,
and in 1992 the United States had a $14 billion trade surplus with Ja-
pan in services, roughly offsetting by 28 percent our $50 billion mer-
chandise deficit.[25]

---

can economy was weakening compared with that of other countries. Nothing, however,
could have been farther from the truth. The U.S. share of total world exports went from
12.3 percent in 1985 to 12.7 percent in 1989. See James J. Cramer, "Heavy Metal: The
Revival of American Manufacturing," *The New Republic,* 27 April 1992.

23. See Ira C. Magaziner and Robert B. Reich, *Minding America's Business* (New
York: Harcourt, Brace, Jovanovitch, 1982).

24. This cost and quality advantage emerges from something called "learning curve
economies." As a manufacturer's total lifetime production of a particular product dou-
bles, its cost per unit tends to be halved because of efficiencies associated with experience in the production of that particular product. The whole phenomenon of learning
curve economies was first discovered and explained by The Boston Consulting Group
and a detailed presentation of their findings can be found in the *Perspectives* pamphlet
series published by The Group.

25. See "U.S. Service Exports Are Growing Rapidly, but Almost Unnoticed," *Wall
Street Journal,* 21 April 1993, 1.

My own office is a good example of a high-technology, knowledge-intensive plant that produces services. In the twenty years I have served as an appellate judge, technology has doubled productivity. The West Virginia Supreme Court is not only the busiest appellate court in the United States on a per-judge basis (because West Virginia does not have an intermediate court of appeals), but it is also the most efficient. We handle more than 3,500 cases a year with five judges. By the third Friday in July of every year, we have usually decided every case ever submitted to us since the beginning of time.

Rarely does a case take more than ten weeks from oral argument to full written opinion in our court. We decided more than three times as many cases in 1992 as we did in 1973, and the cases we decided by full opinion in 1992 were generally more complicated than the cases we decided in 1973. Yet, while our output tripled, we have only doubled our staff, and we work much less hard now than we did in 1973 when I first became a judge. Now I find my job an unmixed pleasure, but during the first ten years I was a judge, I spent many nights, almost a quarter of my Saturdays, and many Sundays in the office. Now I never stay late, and I never come in on a weekend, although I accomplish more work of better quality than I did in 1973.

The reason for my greatly improved personal life has nothing to do with my learning how to be a more efficient judge or how to write opinions more quickly; my improved personal life has to do exclusively with advances in technology. The word processing computer has made child's play of what was once mind-numbing paper production. I regularly prepare between six and twelve drafts of opinions; twenty years ago my secretaries had to retype an entire opinion from scratch every time I made any change. Now, I can rewrite or rearrange a thousand words in a seven-thousand-word opinion and have a complete revised draft in less than twenty minutes.

When I began writing books in 1978, I would type first drafts on an old Olympia portable manual typewriter. Then I would mark up my first draft by hand, take the pages to my office, and ask my secretaries to type second and subsequent drafts. When I edited, I would do so on the typed draft, which limited the number of changes to changes I could make over a weekend. Given the laborious nature of this process and the fact that books on serious subjects earn negligible royalties, I would never have written books had I not had subsidized secretarial help.

Now, however, I have an AST lap-top computer equipped with WordPerfect 6.0, and I don't need secretaries at all for writing books. I can edit on the computer screen and do draft after draft without ever printing anything. Although my spelling leaves something to be desired, now, instead of relying on expensive law clerks and secretaries to avoid spelling mistakes, the computer checks my spelling and catches about nine out of ten mistakes. The problem is that learning how to use a lap-top computer equipped with WordPerfect 6.0 requires a lot of basic skills that aren't taught by any employer on the job.

I learned to use a computer quickly because I already knew how to type. This is a small point, but all of the young adults who might now find steady work at fair wages as travel agents, airline clerks, or newspaper reporters will not be hired unless they know how to type, because computers are the primary tool in those jobs. Furthermore, clerical workers who haven't mastered at least the rudiments of spelling won't be able to use a computer spell check because the spell check assumes that the operator can recognize the word he or she wants when the correct spelling appears. Thus, when one writes the word "annuled" (as I just did a few paragraphs back), and the machine tells the operator he made a spelling mistake, the operator must know that the word he wanted to write is "annulled" rather than "annealed," "annuler," "anilide," "annelid," "inhaled," "unallayed," "unallied," "unallowed," "unalloyed," "unhallowed," and "unhealed," all of which the computer will present as possible choices.

In short, economists like Robert Reich and Lester Thurow who advocate more job training at the high school and post high school levels are missing a critical point. Many students emerging from the tenth grade unable to read and calculate are untrainable, either in the last two years of high school or on the job. These children do not lack bare literacy and numeracy skills because our schools can't teach literacy and numeracy, but because they have too many personal problems to be able to learn. Even our worst schools—the ones in Logan County, West Virginia, and inner-city Washington, D.C.—are capable of teaching basic skills. What neither our worst schools nor our best schools are able to do is overcome students' personal problems.

The bottom line, therefore, is that if the advocates of more government-sponsored training are talking about training the bottom half of our labor force to function at high levels in the law industry, the machine tool industry, or the computer maintenance industry, then they are as mad as hatters. Until people know how to read, write, type, calculate, and spell, schemes designed to teach people how to do high-level clerical work, read blueprints, or find complex instructions in manuals so they can repair equipment they've never seen before will fail.

When Americans farmed, mined coal by hand, manufactured steel, and tightened bolts on assembly lines, lack of basic skills didn't make much difference. Now, as Figure 1 demonstrates, America can maintain its position as the world's highest wage producer only if we move quickly to high-productivity, knowledge-intensive industry. It is upon the roughly 17 plus percent of our population engaged in manufacturing and the export of services (computer software, insurance, and banking, for example) that our country's living standards compared with the rest of the world depend.

Foreign products may dominate K-Mart, but we still get our hair cut, our physical examinations, our newspapers, our houses, our government services (roads, schools, police, and fire protection), our national defense, our recreation, our television programs, our car repairs, and most of our food from other Americans. Because foreign workers can't emigrate to the United States to compete with American workers in industries that must be local, a high-wage, high-profit manufacturing and service exporting sector will favorably affect the terms of trade for all other American workers like barbers, doctors, newspaper journalists, house contractors, government workers, military personnel, ski resort workers, television announcers, and garage mechanics who are not directly involved in international competition. The more foreign currency (yen, deutchmarks, francs, and pounds) our export sector generates through selling goods abroad, the more cheap foreign products everyone in the United States will be able to buy.

Among those who regularly chew over these matters there is a nagging fear that the bottom 10 percent of the American labor force may not be smart enough to find work of any type in the economy of the future. Yet the history of automation reveals that there are always jobs driving trucks, waiting tables, delivering mail, sorting files, entering data, cleaning houses, building structures, cutting hair, making roads, and performing repetitive tasks that can't be automated. Consequently, steady employment at a decent, if perhaps not munificent, wage should be available to everyone within the normal intelligence range who has sufficient social skills to get along with other workers. Workers who are quite limited intellectually will still find good work so long as people who are capable of doing better are not competing with these least able workers for hod carrying, dish washing, and car polishing jobs. Indeed, America's low birth rate since the 1970s should once again turn the terms of trade in favor of low-skill service workers as long as immigration does not increase and the underclass does not expand.

Unfortunately the American underclass—a group characterized by wide-spread illegitimacy, able-bodied unemployment, drug abuse, prostitution, welfare dependency, and crime as a socially accepted means of acquiring ready cash—is expanding. The underclass began growing in the 1960s and has continued to grow at an accelerating rate since then. In the 1960s we inaugurated a host of poverty programs, yet the underclass grew relentlessly. In the 1980s we cut back on all poverty programs from public housing to AFDC, yet the underclass still grew.

The underclass is not just a big-city, minority problem. A large white underclass has spread across heartland America, and increasingly the children of the solid blue-collar class and the middle class fall into the underclass. This descent by the children of functioning parents to the bottom of society occurs because today's children receive much less investment in them than their parents received.

Government antipoverty programs have failed, and would have failed had they been funded at three times their actual levels, because in functioning families the private investment in children dwarfs anything the government is able to do to compensate for lack of that private investment. Focusing our attention on the endemic poverty of never-married, single mothers or the reduction in money income for mothers and children after divorce—particularly when fathers don't pay child support—blinds us to the extent to which the most important investment in children is parental time, not cash money.

Poverty in the United States was far more dire and far more wide-spread in the early years of the Great Depression than it is now, yet the underclass, as I define it, was not growing. In those days, children had even less food, less housing, less medical care, and fewer clothes than they have today, yet they had much more adult time. Lack of a father through illegitimate birth and family disruption through divorce both severely impair a child's ability to prepare academically for high-skill work.[26] A succession of live-in boy friends, live-in girl friends, step parents, step-siblings, and then a renewed cycle of live-ins and steps is not conducive to emotional stability and a focus on educational and work goals.

The slow, steady decline in private investment in our children has been defended rhetorically by resort to terms like "personal liberation," "personal fulfillment," and "empowerment." However, rhetoric probably followed technology: Before technology opened millions of high paying jobs to women, the opportunity cost of mothers' long hours with young children was comparatively low. Now the same amount of time spent with toddlers costs a parent (usually the mother) a hefty market wage, particularly if the parent is single and the taxes are low. Widespread market-sector jobs for women have raised the opportunity costs of quality child care, and quality child care has correspondingly declined. That means a precipitous decline in our total investment in children.

All of the public discussion about inadequate AFDC payments and deadbeat fathers who don't pay child support has tended to focus attention on the "poverty" of children in terms of money and the things money can buy—food, housing, clothes, medical insurance, and recreation. However, the total cost of food, housing, clothes, medical insurance, and recreation pales in comparison to the opportunity cost of a full-time adult nurturing and supervising the child. If we merely assign an arbitrary value of state minimum wage to the necessary adult care-giving hours needed for each family group of preschool children, we come up with an opportunity cost for that care of about $30,000 a year. Because this figure remains roughly the same whether we are looking at a one-child family or a four-child family, substantial economies of scale are achieved in large families where care can be flexibly shared.[27]

26. For a well-written popular review of the most recent scientific literature on the effects of illegitimate birth and divorce on children, see Barbara Dafoe Whitehead, "Dan Quayle Was Right," *The Atlantic* (April 1993).

27. As a result of the Vietnam War and a stint teaching law in China, I have spent considerable time in Asia. Today there are villages in China that are within a hundred miles of Shanghai where the type of food, clothing, medical attention, and recreation available to our poorest, single-mother welfare client would be considered untold luxury. Yet these villages have none of the pathologies we associate in this country with welfare-dependent, underclass life. Sociologists are fond of explaining this away by

Jay Belsky, a professor of clinical psychology at Pennsylvania State University, studies the effects of day care. He has discovered a strong correlation between early, extensive, low-quality day care and subsequent aggressive, noncompliant behavior in school-age children.[28] Thus we return to a labor force incapable of being trained for knowledge-intensive industry. When children are aggressive and noncompliant during the crucial first six years of primary school, school failure becomes imminent. If a child doesn't read well by sixth grade, the child will almost inevitably develop a bad self-image, adopt a negative attitude toward school, and fall farther and farther behind. At that point the child becomes a candidate for the underclass, notwithstanding the possibly solid middle-class status of his or her parents.

"Early day care" means day care during the first year of life; "extensive day care" means day care for more than twenty hours a week. However, the primary determinant of day care's effect on children is quality, and quality is determined by the level of one-on-one interaction between the care provider and the child. Professor Belsky has found that when day-care quality is good, day care can actually be preferable to parental care, particularly if the parents are depressed, self-absorbed, or indifferent.

Emphasizing the fact that high-quality day care can be as effective as parental care, however, distracts us from reality: the day care that is actually available is generally of surpassingly low quality. Working- and middle-class parents who don't live close to relatives find it difficult to procure high-quality day care on a sustained basis. In those

---

pointing out that feelings of deprivation and inferiority are relative. In a very poor society where everyone is poor, nobody feels inferior. There is, of course, some validity to this explanation, but it is at best a partial explanation of why such poor children in other societies are so healthy emotionally and the societies have such low crime rates compared to ours.

The real difference, from my observation, between the Chinese village and an American underclass neighborhood is that in the Chinese village parents and collateral relatives still invest enormous amounts of adult time in the village's children, whereas here some combination of absent fathers, self-absorbed or infantile mothers trying to get their own lives together, and drug and alcohol abuse usually prevents a similar investment of adult time in the typical poor American child.

28. Jay Belsky, "Developmental Risks Associated with Infant Day Care: Attachment Insecurity, Noncompliance, and Aggression?" in *Psychosocial Issues in Day Care,* ed. Shahla S. Chehrazi (Washington, D.C.: American Psychiatric Press, Inc., 1990), and "Day Care Issues," a paper presented at the Conference on Family Journalism organized by the Rockford Institute's Center on Family in America, Arlington, Va., Dec. 1992.

parts of the United States where large numbers of illegal immigrants reside, middle-class parents can hire immigrant nannies. These workers are cheaper than citizens or legal immigrants because the employer need not pay the employer's share of the social security tax, and the worker can be paid less because her wage is not reduced by state and federal tax withholdings.[29]

In general, immigrants provide high-quality day care according to Professor Belsky's criteria; even when they are illiterate and don't speak English (after all, the child is illiterate and doesn't speak English), they interact constantly with the child to develop the child's intellectual and motor skills. Notably, an illegal immigrant day-care worker will cost $6,240 a year even if the worker earns only $3 an hour and no social security taxes are paid. Double-earner, middle-class couples can afford such a sum; most single-earners and working-class couples can't.

Unfortunately, parents who can afford to hire a local woman to care for their child or children in a private house often opt instead for a commercial, impersonal day-care center, with its brightly colored carpets, rooms full of toys, and outwardly cheerful atmosphere. What young parents frequently fail to appreciate is that the quality of equipment and the credentials of the staff are not nearly as important as the level of personal interaction between the care-giver and the child and the stability of relationships likely to be established between the care-giver and the child.

In infant day care, twenty-nine states require no more than a four-to-one ratio of day-care workers to children, while only three states—Kansas, Maryland, and Massachusetts—mandate a three-to-one ratio. Most of the remaining states have five-to-one or six-to-one ratios. If we look at how much care an infant needs, we can easily see why Jay Belsky's analysis is inherently reasonable, even in circumstances where the ratio of children to care-givers is only four to one. Children will require feeding about every three hours; children will require ten minutes for diapering about every two hours; and the care-giver will need to wash her hands thoroughly and sanitize the area after changing each baby.

In an eight-and-a-half-hour day, a care-giver working under the typ-

---

29. All of this, of course, is entirely illegal and leaves the employer open to some very expensive lawsuits if the worker ever gets citizenship.

ical four-to-one ratio will have sixteen diapers to change and twelve feedings to give. As Dorothy Conniff, the director of community services in Madison, Wisconsin, and an experienced executive in the day-care industry points out, four diaper changes and three feedings apiece is not an inordinate amount of care over a long day from the babies' point of view.[30] Yet, even the requisite minimum level of care allows the care-giver little time for the type of quality interaction that Professor Belsky says is essential for appropriate development.

Where the ratio of children to care-giver is only four to one, the care-giver must devote four hours to feeding the babies; two hours and forty minutes to changing them; and, if two and a half minutes are allowed after each change for handwashing and sanitizing the area, another forty minutes to handwashing and cleaning the area. (It is little wonder, with the need to wash hands sixteen times a day or more, that epidemics of diarrhea and related diseases are rampant in day-care centers.) Because feeding and diaper changing are necessarily one-on-one activities, each infant is bound to be largely unattended during the five-plus hours that the other three babies are being attended to. The situation is not much better for toddlers. With a 30 percent a year nationwide turnover in low-paid day-care personnel, staffs are inexperienced, not terribly imaginative, and frequently downright punitive toward their charges.[31]

Professor Belsky summarizes what constitutes high-quality day care:

> The most important thing to children, be they in day care of the care of their parents, is the way in which they are treated. Children tend to thrive, both emotionally and intellectually, when they are cared for by persons who are emotionally invested in them; when the care they receive is sensitive and responsive to their individual needs and desires; and when the caregivers in question have enduring relationships with the children. This is as true of day care as it is of family care.
>
> It is principally because of this final characteristic of quality care that I mentioned—namely the enduringness of relationships—that I take issue with those who criticize me for raising

30. Dorothy Conniff, "Day Care: A Grand and Troubling Social Experiment," *Utne Reader* (May-June 1993).
31. Conniff, "Day Care."

concerns about day care in America and point out, in defense of their criticism, that nonmaternal care is normative in those aboriginal societies considered to be our most accurate reflection of the natural state of the human family. [But] . . . central to these so-called primitive societies are child care arrangements that involve not only parental surrogates who will know the child for his or her entire life, but caregivers who are likely to be blood relatives of the parents and, even if not, have long-standing relationships with the parents that can be expected to continue long after the child needs supplementary care.

[N]othing is likely to be more anomalous with regard to the historical record concerning the human condition and the rearing of children than handing children over, at ever younger ages, for ever longer periods of time, to persons with whom parents do not have long-standing relationships and who are not likely to care for the child for a particularly long period of time or continue to have contact with the family beyond the period when intensive surrogate child care is required.[32]

Although Jay Belsky does not attempt to quantify the relationship between early and extensive day care and subsequent behavior problems, he predicts that if eight or more students in a typical third grade class have had early and extensive day care, the teacher's job will center in class management rather than in teaching. Thus, aggressive, noncompliant behavior on the part of a substantial part of a grade school's student body intensifies the problems for any one child.

As more and more lower-middle class and blue-collar families resort to early and extensive day care of low quality (partially because young parents have moved away from their own parents and collateral kin), the schools that these emotionally crippled children attend will steadily deteriorate, and the quality of workers those schools turn out will become poorer and poorer. This, in turn, will have the effect of widening the income gap between the bottom half of the labor force and the top half of the labor force at the same time that millions of high-skill jobs go begging.[33] The decreasing competence of our labor force

32. Belsky, "Day Care Issues," 6, 7.
33. At the end of 1992, when the *Wall Street Journal* wrote about prospects for 1993, it pointed out that "[u]nemployment probably will continue relatively high be-

due to the lack of parental investment in human capital cannot be made up for by the government, no matter how flush welfare and education budgets become. This is what I call the economic collapse.

Obviously, it is not possible for every mother with a young child to stay at home, yet it is important that we change the stories we tell one another about day care and the value of outside work in comparison to work inside the home. Because the best day care comes from relatives or others who care deeply about a child, a reevaluation of the weight we give to staying in our home area when we decide what jobs we will take must be made. Average day care should be avoided if at all possible when high-quality day care is neither available nor affordable.

As evidence mounts that early and extensive low-quality day care is dangerous, there are still those who manipulate data to downplay the disastrous consequences for children of the day care most people can afford. For example, during the late eighties, sixteen social science professors collaborated on a book on child development. [34] These researchers used impenetrable jargon and unrepresentative data (they focused on upper-middle-class women like themselves) to demonstrate that women who work outside the home nurture young children as effectively as women who do not. No one—particularly Professor Belsky—disagrees with the proposition that this can be the case. The real question is whether, on balance, the mothers who work outside the home actually are as effective at nuturing as mothers who remain at home. The answer to this question is a resounding "no."

It is thus not entirely surprising that even this strange study ended by corroborating Professor Belsky's conclusions, although in a back-handed, jargon-filled way. The crucial finding reads as follows, "[W]here significance occurred [i.e., bad effects on children], the trends showed more favorable developmental or environmental outcomes to be associated with higher maternal occupational status, more favorable attitudes, and higher maternal availability and less

---

cause employers will remain under intense pressure to hold down costs, including their payrolls, and *because of a mismatch between available jobs and job-hunters' skills"* [emphasis added]. This is simply another way of saying that the bottom end of the American labor force has been so badly educated in basic skills that employers cannot begin to train unemployed workers for high-skill operations.

34. A. E. Gottfried and A. W. Gottfried, eds., *Maternal Employment and Child Development* (New York: Plenum Press, 1988).

stress due to dual responsibilities."[35] Stripped of the gibberish, this means that where mothers have high-status, low-stress, and well-paid jobs that don't require very much work or even regular attendance, their children don't suffer.

But high-status, low-stress, easy jobs are not what most working mothers have. When I practiced law, my child support clients used to work eight-hour shifts for barely twice minimum wage down at the local automobile headlight manufacturing plant, where the temperature on the shop floor seldom dipped below 100 degrees, even in the winter. By the time those women commuted home and did the chores, they didn't have much energy left for taking up slack left by a low-quality day-care provider or for disciplining strong-willed teenagers, nor did they have much time for helping children with homework. That was why my child support clients' children were often also my clients in assorted criminal matters.

Books such as *Maternal Employment and Child Development* are one reason why the underclass is burgeoning; the sonorous voices of the upper-middle, college-educated classes dominate the popular media, but these folks speak for a small minority of the population. The problems of surgeons married to tenured professors of history, the problems of lawyers married to one another, and the problems of computer engineers married to architects are not the problems of at least 90 percent of the American population.

Although the fact is obvious, it appears to escape notice by most popular commentators that double-income, college-educated couples can afford high-quality day care (given by people like Zoë Baird's famous illegal Hispanic nanny) and can also afford to live in rich neighborhoods where a high proportion of families still have only one worker—the husband. Double-income, college-educated couples need not cope with their children's exposure to peers who come to school with such severe family-related pathologies that the youngsters constitute a serious threat to other students' safety every day, nor need such favored couples cope with their children playing in neighborhoods devoid of adult supervision during all the weekday hours when children are home from school. For the average person who must cope with these problems, however, the advent of socially acceptable alter-

35. Gottfried and Gottfried, eds., *Maternal Employment and Child Development*, 55.

native family structures has not been a "liberating," "self-fulfilling," or "empowering" event.

It is hard to say all of these things in a straightforward way without sounding smug, judgmental, and callous. The women clients I represented in child support cases were wonderful people who worked hard and did the best they could under difficult circumstances. I do not describe what is now happening to women like the ones I used to represent or to their children in such a tactless way because I want to be gratuitously critical of struggling people. Rather, I simply want to reverse the trends that are destroying the bottom half of our labor force. No government policies of any stripe can help raise living standards until we come to grips with family structure problems. And just how irresponsible our private behavior has waxed, albeit unintentionally, will become obvious in chapter 5.

5

The Social Collapse

This book emerged from the least controversial of all possible undertakings for a judge—an effort to lower the crime rate. When I thought
that our crime problem might be solved by more aggressive patrolling,
I wrote a book titled *Take Back Your Neighborhood: A Case for Modern-day "Vigilantism,"* which suggested entirely lawful, unarmed,
community policing as a way to augment professional officers and
make crime control efforts less reactive and more active.[1] In many
places where the criminals are juvenile delinquents, amateur drug
dealers, and standard housebreakers, community patrolling by unarmed volunteers can be successful. However, in the places with the
highest crime rates—particularly major cities—the whole community
patrolling concept is, at best, a misinformed idea. I didn't understand
how stupid the idea was until Random House sent me around the
country during 1991 to promote the paperback version of the book.

During that trip, people described their neighborhoods to me, related the actions to which they and their neighbors had resorted to
halt street crimes and housebreakings, and communicated their terror
in the face of the accelerating savagery they saw all around them. Most
of these frightened people unhesitatingly admitted their staunch unwillingness to engage in any type of unarmed community patrolling.[2]

It was from this reasonably intensive, on-the-ground education in
Atlanta, Washington, New York, Chicago, Denver, Portland, and Seat-
tle, as well as long conversations by telephone on hour-long radio call-
in shows from cities like Houston, Los Angeles, Miami, and San Anto-
nio, that I realized the utter impossibility of law enforcement—either

1. Richard Neely, *Take Back Your Neighborhood: A Case for Modern-day "Vigilantism"* (New York: Donald I. Fine, 1990).
2. Armed community patrolling has too many dangers to be a viable option for neighborhood volunteers.

public or private—preventing the relentless rise in the crime rate we are now witnessing.[3] Draconian measures bandied about to solve the problem of repeat offenders—widespread capital punishment or incarceration of felons for long terms in rural prison camps, where inmates either work to grow food and provide for their own shelter or are allowed to die—would sound the death knell for civil rights and civil liberties as we know them.

Thus I do not write this book out of a sense of morality, nostalgia, or a desire to share my personal vision of proper domestic life. I write this book because the need to control crime and violence is urgent. Ten years of trying to make police, prosecutors, courts, and prisons work[4] through investigations into crime control have led me down such blind alleys as community patrolling, specialized courts to handle violent crime, and cheap ways to incapacitate convicted felons for long periods, yet at every turn I have been drawn back to the relationship between unstable families and accelerating crime. Wadud Ahmad, a black student at Philadelphia's Temple University, summarized anecdotally the relationship between family structure and crime, which all of us who see criminals every day have observed for years: "I'm one of the only ones among my peers in high school who's alive and doesn't have a record," he said. "I'm not any different from them, but I came from an Islamic household. My parents were very strict. Outside the house, I was with the guys on the corner."[5]

The radio call-in shows I did in 1991 to talk about crime in cities like Houston and Chicago put in plain words the fact that people do not patrol their own neighborhoods or confront the bad guys in any way, both because they are afraid and because the communities with the most serious crime problems lack the cohesion to organize for self-defense. The callers also made plain that in most of America where

3. Although population has increased only 41 percent since 1960, the number of violent crimes has increased more than 500 percent, and total crimes have increased over 300 percent. The rate of violent crime in the United States is higher than in any other industrialized country. Eight out of every ten Americans will be a victim of violent crime at least once in their lives. See William J. Bennett, *The Index of Leading Cultural Indicators* (Washington, D.C.: Empower America, The Heritage Foundation, and Free Congress Foundation, 1993).

4. In 1984 I wrote a book titled *Why Courts Don't Work* (New York: McGraw Hill), which didn't lower the crime rate by even one purse snatching but did help me figure out where many of the blind alleys in crime control are located.

5. Quoted by Nicholas Lemann, "Black Nationalism on Campus," *The Atlantic* (Jan. 1993): 44.

community crime control with unarmed patrols might actually work, the high labor force participation rate makes organized patrolling and active vigilance nearly impossible because people are overwhelmed by the time demands of their jobs, commuting, and the chores of daily life.

There is little that police, courts, or prisons can do to prevent violent crime because serious villainy is almost entirely a function of social class and family background. For example, West Virginia, forty-ninth among the states in per capita income,[6] has the country's lowest crime rate. West Virginia's court system is extraordinarily efficient by national standards, but the crime rate is not low because the courts work; rather, the courts work because the crime rate is low. Much as I would like to take credit for West Virginia's stellar performance on the law and order front, the truth is that our low crime rate emerges naturally from our small towns, where people know one another and one another's children, and from our very low female labor force participation rate, which ensures that our children receive above-average care.

Although we have a lot of divorce and illegitimacy in West Virginia, we also have large, extended families that provide concerned care providers for children, even when the children are illegitimate, the parents are divorced, or both of the parents work full time. I know for sure that there is nothing that we in state government in West Virginia are doing that is particularly right to keep our crime rate low, just as I suspect that there is nothing that New York City is doing in its government that is particularly wrong to keep its crime rate high.

Crime has nothing to do with what governments do, or even with such things as easy availability of guns. West Virginians, for example, have one of the highest rates of gun ownership in the United States,

6. In fairness, I should probably point out that comparing West Virginia's income level to the rest of the country's income level is like comparing American wage rates to French or Japanese wage rates. If you measure the average West Virginian's income by what he or she can buy with his or her wage in New York, Washington, or Los Angeles, then the average West Virginian is very poor indeed. If, however, you measure the average West Virginian's income by what he or she can buy in West Virginia, then the average West Virginian is much richer than the average New Yorker, Washingtonian, or Los Angeleno. In general, West Virginians have short commutes, don't need private schools, and don't need to spend a lot of money protecting themselves from crime. This has bearing on my discussion later in this chapter of how crime is a function of growing up in conditions of poverty and deprivation. "Deprivation" largely has to do with how you think that you are doing in comparison to other people living around you.

and West Virginia's state constitution guarantees everyone the right to carry a rifle or pistol openly on public streets. Yet our rate of homicide with firearms is very low, and our rate of death among bystanders accidently shot in cross fires is nearly zero. Washington, D.C., in contrast, has such strict gun control that a law-abiding citizen is prohibited from keeping a firearm of any sort in his or her own home for self-defense, yet a person's likelihood of being shot to death in Washington, D.C., exceeds either his or her likelihood of being killed in an automobile accident or of dying of cancer.

Likewise, both Scotland and Canada have extraordinarily strict gun control laws, yet both have firearm-related crime rates substantially higher than Switzerland, where every able-bodied male citizen over the age of twenty is required to be in the military reserve and is required by law to keep his personal military weapon—pistol or rifle—in his house.[7] Furthermore, Swiss soldiers are given their pistols and rifles when they retire from the military reserve, which puts millions of old weapons in private hands in Switzerland.

Among persons of good will who want government to lend everyone a helping hand, discussions of crime tend to center in "root causes," such as poor housing, bad education, and lack of jobs, more than in strict laws, better policing, and severer sentencing. To the extent that the root causes lobby is unwilling to take on the critical issue of family structure, however, they are wasting their time. As I indicated earlier, large numbers of service jobs that pay more than double state minimum wage go begging in big cities because young, unemployed males prefer crime and street life to work. And, if bad schools and poor housing were the preeminent cause of crime, West Virginia would certainly not have the lowest crime rate in the United States.

Nationally, more than 70 percent of all juveniles in state reform

7. See David B. Kopel, *The Samurai, the Mountie, and the Cowboy* (Buffalo: Prometheus Books, 1992), 407. In February 1993, I spent a day visiting the Swiss army artillery training camp at Sion to observe firsthand the types of weapons Swiss soldiers keep at home. Swiss infantrymen are issued high-powered, heavy caliber, fully automatic assault rifles that are far more lethal than the American army's M-16 that was used by our troops in Vietnam. Swiss artillerymen are issued a lighter, fully automatic defensive rifle that is of slightly smaller caliber. Both of these weapons have "selector switches" that allow the soldier to determine whether he will fire the weapon like a machine gun or one round at a time. However, when the soldier takes his weapon home for safe-keeping, the company armorer locks the weapon in the "semi-automatic" position (i.e., the weapon will fire only one bullet at a time) with a key device that only the official armorer is allowed to use. The fact that any schoolboy knows how to modify a locked weapon to make it fully automatic renders this protective measure entirely cosmetic.

schools come from fatherless homes. In test after test, even after the groups of subjects are controlled for income, boys from single-mother homes are significantly more likely than others to commit crimes and wind up in the juvenile justice system. We incarcerate a higher percentage of our population than any other advanced industrial country because we have the highest level of single-mother families (both divorced and never-married) than any other advanced industrial country. Indeed, studies show that the relationship between crime and family structure is so strong that controlling for family configuration erases any relationship between race and crime and low income and crime.[8]

There are at least half a billion decidedly law-abiding citizens in heartland China who live on incomes so meager that a New York or Washington welfare client's household would appear to them as opulent as that of a fabled maharajah. In the United States, crime does increase in direct proportion to geographical concentrations of poverty, but crime varies little or not at all with fluctuations in the economic cycle. Therefore, it is not poverty itself that makes criminals, but rather a complex concatenation of social habits and attitudes that emerge from growing up and living in conditions of poverty and deprivation. In this last regard, China and West Virginia have certain similarities. Although West Virginia may appear poor on the national charts, people don't feel particularly poor when they compare themselves to their neighbors, which is why West Virginians—unlike Washington or Los Angeles slum dwellers—aren't caught up in emotional problems arising from perceived deprivation.

Careful analysis of crime statistics demonstrates that violent crime rates are (1) highest against black males overall; (2) higher against blacks than whites or members of other minority groups; (3) higher against unemployed persons—whether male, female, white, or black—than against employed persons in their respective groups; (4) higher against males than females; and (5) lowest against white females.[9] In the words of a small-town cop who years ago tried to explain law enforcement to me, all these statistics mean that "crime happens where the criminals are at."

Violent criminals tend to be single males between the ages of four-

8. See Barbara Dafoe Whitehead, "Dan Quayle Was Right," *The Atlantic* (April 1993).

9. U.S. Department of Justice, Office of Justice Programs, Bureau of Justice Statistics, *BJS Data Report* (Washington: U.S. Government Printing Office, 1988).

teen and twenty-seven, although the most serious crime is disproportionately perpetrated by males between the ages of seventeen and
twenty-four. The most likely victims of crime, then, are the people
who regularly live, work, or socialize in proximity to young, uneducated, unemployed males. Men with families are much less likely to be
violent criminals than single men. In fact, the correlation between
marriage and a reluctance to engage in criminal behavior is so pronounced that many probation departments strenuously encourage
marriage between their male and female clients. Even marriages between convicted felons tend to reduce significantly the disposition on
the part of both spouses to commit crimes.

All respectable research leads to the ineluctable conclusion that
nothing short of a far higher proportion of stable two-parent homes
than currently exists in America will provide the conditions necessary
to stabilize and then slowly lower the crime rate. Pie in the sky solutions like stricter gun control, more policing (unless we become a
police state), and longer sentences would have negligible effects on
the total level of violent crime.

Those who believe that strict gun control will keep automatic
weapons out of the hands of felons need look only at the drug industry to see how supply and demand forces inevitably confound any serious effort to control contraband that people want to buy. The quan-
tity of drugs illegally imported into the United States increases
significantly every year in spite of massive efforts to keep drugs out.
Cocaine wholesale prices in the United States dropped from $55,000
per kilo in 1980 to $15,000 per kilo in mid-1988. As University of
Michigan researcher Lloyd Johnston noted in April 1988, "The supply
of cocaine has never been greater in the streets, the price has never
been lower, and [the] drug has never been purer."

Given the length of America's borders, the lack of personnel in the
U.S. Customs Service, and our unwillingness to adopt sanctions like
capital punishment, our experience with drugs demonstrates that
even if we repealed the Second Amendment, we could not control the
importation and distribution of illegal guns. This is what the saner
anti-gun-control zealots are concerned about when they oppose a
tightening of qualifications for legal firearms purchase because they
fear that law-abiding citizens will adhere to gun control rules while the
criminals will ignore them and buy cheap guns from illegal importers.
No sooner would we institute strict national gun control than foreign-

ers would exploit the high profits available in an illegal market (as they have in drugs) to start whole new low-tech industries manufacturing Saturday night specials. Although strict waiting periods and detailed background checks, as are currently suggested by the saner pro-gun-control zealots, would reduce the number of weapons in the hands of impulsive crazies and would reduce marginally the number of heat-of-passion killings, gun control would have little or no effect on the number of weapons in the hands of professional criminals, particularly because even today a high percentage of weapons used in crimes have been stolen from persons possessing weapons legally.

Solutions like gun control and longer sentences are proposed and seriously discussed only because few people understand the sociology of crime and the politics of public law enforcement.[10] According to a classic study by the staff of the *New York Times* in January 1981 (which remains highly representative of what happens in all major cities), hardly any of the persons arrested on felony charges in New York City are ever prosecuted and convicted as felons. New York Police Department figures showed that the chances of a person arrested for a felony being sentenced to prison was one in 108. Although police "overcharging" explains many of these cases, avoidances of prison sentences overwhelmingly may be traced to prosecuting authorities' willingness to permit felons to plead guilty to lesser charges, a direct function of both the limited judicial resources available to give jury trials and the chronic understaffing of the prosecutors' offices. In 1979 there were 104,413 felony arrests in New York City, of which 88,095 cases were dismissed and 16,318 indictments procured. Of those indicted, 56 percent pled guilty to felonies (but often less severe felonies than those with which they were originally charged), 16 percent pled guilty to misdemeanors, 12 percent were dismissed after indictment, only 13 percent went to jury trial, and 3 percent resulted in some other disposition.

These figures remain instructive in that they were collected at a time when New York State was reasonably solvent. When, in 1990 the budget crises in New York forced legislators and the governor to reduce all budgets in order to keep the state afloat, the executive and legislature decreased the courts' budget by 4 percent for the next

10. For a detailed discussion of the political limits to public law enforcement, see Neely, *Take Back Your Neighborhood,* ch. 3.

fiscal year, laying off 1,700 personnel of the courts' nonjudicial staff.[11] No judges received pink slips, but the lack of court personnel rendered them idle and unproductive and effectively confined them to chambers. The plan to give priority in rationed funds to criminal, family, and housing matters under the budget cutting scheme did not work. Ultimately, the governor and the chief justice agreed to appropriate sufficient funds in the 1992-93 judicial budget to restore the 1,700 staff positions that had been eliminated, but the settlement left the court budget only more or less as it was in 1990-91. It did not give the courts the 4 percent increase they had requested in 1991-92 to handle their additional case load. Thus, since the *New York Times's* study things have gotten worse and not better in New York, a pattern largely representative of all American urban, industrial states.

In the real world of tight public budgets and widespread antipathy to police, facile proposals to "get tough on crime" don't offer any fairer prospects of success than the well-meaning babble of the root causes lobby. Appealing proposals to increase the number of police—particularly the number of police actively patrolling the streets—fails to appreciate the prohibitive expense of using uniformed police officers on the scale this society now requires. It costs at least $42,000 a year to put a uniformed officer on the street in a typical small heartland American city when we include the officer's pension, disability insurance, equipment, and supporting personnel. Unless one is unrealistic enough to believe that major new taxes will be imposed to support law enforcement, then the money for additional police must come from schools, social welfare, highways, or health. Once these options are explained, no one is about to rob those programs to finance more cops, including even those demanding more cops.

Increases in the number of police (short of the type of police presence associated with a police state) have never reduced the crime rate. Between 1954 and 1974, the size of the New York City Police Department grew by 54 percent while the civilian population of the city remained nearly constant. The rate of crime, however, appreciated faster than the police. This same phenomenon is present in different forms across the country, where an increase in the numbers of police over short periods corresponded with little reduction in crime.

11. See John K. Powers, "Crisis in the Courts? The New York Experience," *Trial* (April 1993).

In 1965, one of the most important experiments in policing ever done was conducted in the New York subway system. For the two years before 1965, crime in the subways rose by about 50 percent a year. In April 1965, Mayor Robert Wagner, resolving to provide one officer for every train and another for every station between the hours of 8 P.M. and 4 A.M.—the times of highest crime—ordered an increase in transit police force from 1,200 officers to just over 3,100. The effect of this increase in manpower over an eight-year period have been used by just about everyone in the crime control business to prove just about every proposition anyone wants to prove.

In a nutshell, New York City found that immediately after the introduction of the additional transit police, crime rates fell dramatically in the subways. But within a year or so, the number of subway robberies began to rise again rapidly. By 1970 there were six times as many robberies as had occurred in 1965 before the addition of the new officers. Indeed, the number of subway felonies per hour during the night fell in 1965 and remained low, while the number of felonies during the day (after a brief decrease in 1965 immediately following publicity concerning the new officers) increased steadily from 1965 on. Investigators from the New York City Rand Institute concluded that although subway crime has tended to rise in general over the years, the addition of uniformed officers to the trains and stations during the evening hours has caused a significant reduction in crime during those hours.[12]

In short, although crime can be reduced in any confined area by heavy patrolling, the need to commit crime on the part of professional criminals and drug addicts inevitably moves their crimes from areas of heavy patrols to areas of light patrols. That bored teenagers and other amateur criminals, in contrast, are probably not displaced means that patrolling can have a net positive effect (in the same way that some types of pistol control can have a net positive effect) but not a sufficiently positive effect to overcome today's relentless rise in the rate of violent crime.

The failure of police to control crime, in spite of substantial argumentation in their numbers, lies the way modern police operate—that is, their "reactive" rather than "active" approach to law enforcement.

12. James Q. Wilson, *Thinking about Crime,* rev. ed. (New York: Basic Books, 1983), 65.

Indeed, experiments have shown that when massive numbers of police are thrown at a crime problem, and the new personnel do nothing but patrol, there is at least a momentary decline in crime. The problem is that public budgets can't afford this type of active policing across a broad front, and even if substantially more public money were appropriated to police budgets, police departments would also need to revolutionize the way they operate, which is about as likely to happen in the real political world as a major new infusion of funds.

At bottom the crime rate in the United States will continue to rise so long as the primary engine of social control—the family—is in widespread disrepair. The primary difference between American city slum-dwellers, who are both committed criminals and fabulously rich by third world standards, and scrupulously honest Chinese peasants, who are poor by any standard, is family and culture. Indeed, the families in the poor sections of West Virginia, where the crime rate is nonetheless extraordinarily low by American standards, resemble the Chinese more than they do Americans in our inner cities. Like the Chinese, West Virginia families not only control and educate their children within their households, but with one or two working adults, families—unlike never-married, single parents—also try to live in neighborhoods among other families. And, even though their incomes may technically place them below the "poverty line," these families constitute communities that support schools, churches, and other institutions that help mould the young in a positive way.

There is thus a difference between the "working poor"—people who are struggling to support themselves and their families, educate their children, strengthen their communities, and improve their circumstances—and what I call in this book the "underclass." Underclass life, as I explained earlier, is characterized by widespread illegitimacy, able-bodied unemployment, drug abuse, prostitution, welfare dependency, and crime as a socially accepted means of acquiring ready cash. It was largely the underclass to whom I referred in the last chapter when I discussed the failure of Americans for the first time in our history to improve themselves by taking available jobs. Yet I do not want to emphasize the distinctive qualities of the underclass too much, because it appears that many "underclass" ways of doing things are now invading other strata of society. Thus ordinary high school graduate, white American women with dependent children are just one divorce and one disappearing husband away from grinding poverty. Notwithstanding the federal government's efforts to enforce the payment of family support, many fathers simply can't pay. Those who can pay go for years without paying, and most fathers, regardless of their incomes, end up paying far less than they have been ordered to pay by the courts.

There is probably more downward mobility in American society today than at any other time in our history. When self-absorbed, double-income professional parents neglect their children (although for entirely different reasons than those that induce the underclass to neglect their children), the children typically react by taking drugs, failing in school, and joining the street culture, all of which hastens their fall from the middle class into the underclass. When families have money, even negligent parents will usually intercede to protect their children from the most ravaging aspects of underclass life (like living on the street in the South Bronx), but parental assistance will delay the fall from middle-class grace for only one generation.

Among black Americans, the illegitimacy rate is now so high (64 percent)[13] that unless there is a major change in attitudes, ten years will see more than half of all black children living in an exclusively underclass world dominated by a criminal culture.[14] Although the prospects for blacks are, perhaps, the most bleak among our various identifiable social groups, rising divorce and illegitimacy rates guarantee accelerating incidences of downward mobility that dampen the prospect for white children as well. In 1960, 2 percent of all white babies were born to unwed mothers; in 1970, the figure was 6 percent; in 1980, the figure was 11 percent; and by 1992 the figure was roughly 19 percent.[15] Given the proportion of whites to blacks in the total population, a white underclass is in the long run a more prominent hazard in terms of rising crime rates than the black underclass that dominates the current conception of underclass life.

Those Americans who find their lives reasonably free from crime do not owe their safety to the superb police forces of the areas in

13. Table 89, *Statistical Abstract of the United States* (1992).

14. During the twelve months ending in mid-1987, black married women with incomes of more than $15,000 had fewer than 165,000 babies. During the same period, black unwed women with household incomes less than $10,000 (including welfare and other government transfer payments) had 177,000 babies. See M. Kondracke, "The Two Black Americas," *The New Republic,* 6 Feb. 1989.

15. Table 89, *Statistical Abstract of the United States* (1992); *Historical Statistics of the United States: Colonial Times to 1970* (1975).

which they live. Rather, they owe their safety to the fact that they have isolated themselves among other middle- and upper-middle-class neighbors, who, in turn, have virtually no inclinations to rob, burgle, mug, and murder one another. Walled private communities with paid guards, fortresslike city apartment buildings, and ritzy suburbs hours away from the nearest public housing are all prohibitively expensive. Not many law-abiding Americans can afford to live in communities so removed from the criminal underclass that crime is an improbable occurrence. Families earning average incomes have little choice but to live in economically and socially mixed neighborhoods where violent crime and property crime are constant threats. All of this is slowly changing the face of America in imperceptible yet extraordinarily negative ways that take us to a *sauve qui peut* (every man for himself) survival strategy.[16]

Our crime problem is now so acute that we are beginning to build prisons for ourselves instead of the criminals. After all, looked at objectively, the most important function of a prison is to incapacitate criminals so they can't get at us. Therefore, why waste perfectly good and very expensive prisons on criminals when we could live in them ourselves? Good steel doors, fortified walls, and armed guards can keep the criminals out just as effectively as these security devices can keep them in. In the Middle Ages, residents of areas subject to periodic invasion lived in (or at least could retreat to) prisonlike, fortified castles while bands of Vikings or unemployed mercenaries foraged for loot and provisions in the countryside. There were years at a time in those days when a person just couldn't live in an unfortified farm house and be safe, so law-abiding residents lived in prisons and left the rest of the world to the criminals.

In rich American towns like Palm Beach, Florida, where the price of real estate ($2 million dollars an acre and up) effectively excludes both the poor and the middle class, it is possible to have a superb, publicly financed police system. In such a community everyone agrees that the purpose of the police is to keep undesirables out, and in so doing to distinguish between true undesirables and either the employees or customers of the residents. In Palm Beach, local tax lev-

16. The last radio message broadcast by Nazi Germany's military headquarters as the Soviet Army broke through the final lines of defense around Berlin in June 1945 was, ironically, this French phrase repeated over and over by a dedicated radio operator who remained at his post to the end.

ies to prevent crime through active patrolling afford public police officers strong logistical support and hefty salaries. The crime rate is negligible in Palm Beach, and local juries generally support the police in their occasional in-court clashes with the underclass. Even the Palm Beach parking regulations, which limit street parking to those residents with permits, are designed to make it nearly impossible for lower-class nonresidents to linger without paying stiff parking fees, which rich tourists, of course, can easily afford.

A woman who winters in Palm Beach and spends the rest of her time in Washington, D.C., would be reluctant to support Washington's police force as lavishly as she does Palm Beach's. In Washington, such support would simply be money down the drain from her private point of view. Even if her municipal taxes were doubled in Washington, there would be little improvement in her own level of protection. Indeed, because of her private wealth, our Palm Beach snowbird can protect herself when she has to be in Washington far better than the corrupt and lackluster Washington police can protect her. So poor and mismanaged is Washington that in August and September of 1989 the police ran out of kits for preserving evidence in rape cases. When television station WUSA broke the story, the police couldn't understand what all the fuss was about. "We run out of pencils, too," said a department spokesperson. By 1992 the Washington police themselves were being indicted as principle actors in crime rings involving drugs and stolen goods. By 1993, the mayor of Washington requested the federal government to mobilize the National Guard for law enforcement. In short, no one who could do better would want anything to do with a police department so underfunded that it can't even preserve, much less uncover, evidence of serious crimes, and whose investigating officers are as likely as not to be casing the premises they visit in the line of duty for their burglar friends.

A wealthy resident of Washington, then, would naturally want to recreate a replica of Palm Beach right in downtown Murder City so that she would have no need for the official police. The best way to do that would be to create a pleasant little prison through the privatization of space. If the rich woman could find two hundred other rich people, then the safe thing for her to do in Washington would be to custom design a community with a high wall, replete with armed guards to exclude the unwelcome, a tightly monitored entry gate, and active patrols to ensure that nobody successfully penetrated the barriers.

Of course, the regular police engaging in this intrusive type of surveillance, patrolling, and identity checking on public streets would violate constitutional rights. In a private community, in contrast, residents can contract with one another for whatever degree of intrusion they are willing to accept on their own property and then enforce that contract among themselves. These types of arrangements effectively render the absence of such items as publicly funded rape kits a matter of indifference because the residents of such communities are never raped. Thus, private action can and often does solve public problems, but only when there is private money in quantities that working-class Americans can't afford. The middle-class and upper-middle-class answer to crime is not better public policing, but flight.

Once the rich opt out of the public sector—as they largely have with regard to big city public schools—political support for the public sector falters. This has already happened in city law enforcement because those who can afford it now hire private security guards. In fact, private security in the United States has become as strong a growth industry as waste management. The increasing prevalence of limited-access walled communities is the most prominent symptom of our flight from dependence on the public sector and one part of a general trend toward the "privatization" of space. Notably, not all privatization of space is the result of a crime threat. Much privatization, such as shopping malls, emerges from entirely benign considerations like economies of scale. Nonetheless, once space is privatized for any reason, use of private property rights to create an "exclusive" environment naturally becomes the next step.[17]

The urge to "privatize" space has even gone beyond legitimately private space and entered the public sphere. In areas served by public streets we are now beginning to see barricading of neighborhoods exactly like medieval efforts at creating convenient fortified retreats. In sections of Miami and Fort Lauderdale, private guards control checkpoints and lower gates to stop cars. Constitutional objections are met by the argument—erroneous, I believe—that the barricades are

17. During the 1989 Christmas season, for example, there was a major brouhaha in Cleveland, Ohio, over the exclusion of Salvation Army bell ringers from Cleveland's three largest shopping malls. This was a serious blow to the financing of a worthy charitable organization, but the exclusion of solicitors follows logically from the control inherent in shopping mall architecture, where access by public streets is no longer necessary.

lawful because all motorists are detained and, in principle, allowed to enter, after drivers have answered questions and had their license numbers written down.

The results of residential space privatization are spectacular, as evidence from places like Starrett City, a middle-class housing development in Brooklyn, New York, conclusively shows. Starrett City houses roughly twenty thousand people in 5,881 apartments within a three-acre landfill nestled in the crime-ridden area between Canarsie, Brooklyn, and the borough of Queens. Starrett City's security force consists of fifty-five private officers who occasionally use trained dogs on foot patrols. Twenty-seven percent of households have children, 30 percent of residents are senior citizens, and 62 percent are women. A comparison of the crime rates for Starrett City and the surrounding 77th police precinct reveals the following annual rates per one thousand residents: murder—Starrett City .05, police precinct .22; rape—Starrett City .10, police precinct .83; robbery—Starrett City 2.75, police precinct 15.51; aggravated assault—Starrett City 1.05, police precinct 6.88; burglary—Starrett City .40, police precinct 15.64; and vehicular theft—Starrett City 1.10, police precinct 9.51.[18]

These statistics affirm both the entirely class-related nature of crime and the effectiveness of very expensive private police. Starrett City houses exclusively middle-class people, which means that the neighborhood need protect itself against only intruders from outside, and outside intruders are the easiest criminals for a good police force to recognize. Without the private patrols and limited access, however, the middle class would never agree to live in an enclave surrounded by slums.[19]

Both the real privatization of space with limited-access, walled communities patrolled by paid guards and the quasi-privatization of space—such as in Miami and Fort Lauderdale—have an unintended sinister side effect. This side effect is the "displacement" phenomenon to which I earlier alluded in discussing the effect of more police in the New York subways. The aggressive privatization of space by the upper-income groups—whether that privatization occurs in walled neighborhoods like Starrett City, exclusive private schools, or exclusive rec-

18. See L. Klein, J. Luxenburg, and M. King, "Perceived Neighborhood Crime and the Impact of Private Security," *Crime and Delinquency* (July 1989).

19. Klein, Luxenburg, and King, "Perceived Neighborhood Crime and the Impact of Private Security."

reational areas—causes crime and other social problems associated with poor people (such as the disruptive behavior among third-graders because of early and extensive low-quality day care) to be displaced and concentrated in vulnerable poor neighborhoods.

In New York City, car owners have begun entering into contracts with the city police to waive the constitutional rights that protect them from illegal stops, searches, and seizures (those, in other words, made without probable cause) between 1 and 5 in the morning—the hours during which most automobiles are stolen. Motorists who have agreed to this most reasonable waiver arrangement place two yellow decals on their rear windows, indicating a willingness to have their car stopped, searched, and the driver identified for absolutely no reason during nighttime hours. While this project has greatly reduced the theft of vehicles with the yellow stickers, it has had no effect whatsoever on the overall rate of vehicle theft. All the project has done is displace auto theft from those who are willing to waive constitutional rights to those who either are unwilling or don't understand the project.[20]

West Virginia offers a counterexample of what happens when the blue-collar, middle, and upper-middle classes all interact on a daily basis. West Virginia has a few housing projects in the larger cities, and every city has a slum, but the interaction among all social classes is much higher in West Virginia than in the urban states. Most upper-middle-class West Virginians live inside our cities and towns. We have almost no suburban areas because people are unwilling to commute long distances to work; it would not occur to me to live more than ten minutes from my office. In West Virginia, the highest crime rates, as a percentage of the county populations, occur not in our cities but in rural areas, where underclass persons live together in isolated pockets. In short, the increasing separation of successful people from unsuccessful people in urban America due to their fear of crime reinforces pathologies. It is difficult for successful people to be models for unsuccessful people if the two never meet face to face.

There is widespread optimism about the war on drugs because drug usage appears to be declining on a long-term basis in all groups but the underclass. This indeed is a good sign in that it demonstrates

---

20. See G. Marx, "An Increase in Individual Aggressive Countermeasures?" *Crime and Delinquency* (July 1989).

that people may change their attitudes and behavior in response to public information campaigns. Our efforts in the schools and on television with the "just say no!" program, along with public service television and radio commercials (plus heavy-handed propaganda insinuated into teleplays and movies) have paid big dividends. Nonetheless, it would be silly to lose sight of the continued widespread use of drugs among a growing underclass and how that usage, along with the growing market for illegal drugs that an expanding underclass creates, are slowly dehumanizing America.

The greatest allies that foreign drug producers have in the United States are illegitimacy, divorce, and parental neglect. These three factors virtually guarantee a burgeoning underclass of customers. In general, our success in getting people to stop using drugs has been much greater with the higher classes than with the lower classes. The more dysfunctional any person's life becomes, the more likely that person is to use drugs. Consequently, drug usage among teenagers is roughly congruent with instances of incompetent nurture in those teenagers' families. As a general rule, the greater a person's problems, the greater the likelihood that the person will resort to drugs for chemical relief. Therefore, if downward mobility continues at its current unprecedented rate and the underclass continues to grow, that group's increased aggregate use of drugs will offset the downward trend we see in drug use among the blue-collar, middle- and upper-middle classes. Furthermore, in order for the underclass to buy drugs, they must steal.

This chapter does not seek to explore the ins and outs of crime, but rather to show that without a change in the stories we are telling one another about family, work, and child care American society is going to suffer a massive social collapse characterized by ever-expanding crime and violence. That massive collapse is already presaged in our big cities and working-class suburbs, but in order to appreciate just how serious the collapse is likely to be, we must delve into the cycle of family breakdown, downward mobility, drug usage, and then explore how the underclass customers of drug merchants infect American society from top to bottom.

The intrusion of drugs into American culture may be as cataclysmic an event for us as the arrival of marauding bands of unemployed mercenary soldiers discharged from England's war with France was for Italy in the fourteenth century. More than one in ten Americans has used an illegal drug within the last thirty days; seven in ten persons arrested for other offenses test positive for drugs. In addition, the illegal drug industry has spawned violence and savagery on a scale unparalleled in American history. Although street warfare between rival drug gangs is now limited to the inner cities, other drug-related violence moves relentlessly to suburbs, small cities, and rural county seats.

Drug trafficking is so profitable that it invites levels of official corruption that undermine our entire law enforcement apparatus. Corruption has perils that must be offset for a police officer to risk career, pension, and prison, but, unlike ordinary crime, drug profits are big enough to turn the head of all but the most honest officers. And, there is more than enough drug money to go around. Involvement may not include selling drugs or tipping off dealers; just protecting a friend's bar where drugs are sold is sufficient involvement to discourage an officer's moral outrage. In such an atmosphere the lone whistle-blower is likely to have a fatal accident.

People who sell drugs are usually involved in other criminal activities. Consequently, once an officer becomes involved with drug dealers—perhaps justifying his or her conduct on the theory that the dealers are engaged only in "victimless" crime—it is an easy step to collaborating in other criminal enterprises. In a copyrighted story in February 1989, the *Detroit News* reported that for every thousand officers, Detroit police were alleged to have committed 151 crimes each year. Allegations, of course, are cheap, but the *Detroit News,* availing itself of the Michigan Freedom of Information Act, determined that there were 7.2 substantiated allegations against officers in Detroit for every thousand officers.

Other cities that the *News* surveyed for police corruption were New York, with 112.7 unsubstantiated allegations per thousand officers; Los Angeles, with 109.5; Dallas, with 65.6; Houston, with 42.7; Philadelphia, with 20.7; Chicago, with 13.6; and Phoenix, with 10.7. Houston finished first in substantiated allegations, with 12.7 per thousand officers, followed by Dallas, with 10; Los Angeles, with 9.5; New York, with 7.5; and then Detroit. According to the *News,* crimes by police a few years earlier usually involved the use of excessive force. During the late eighties, however, Detroit officers were accused of rape, hiring an arsonist to set fire to an occupied apartment building, car theft, insurance fraud, cocaine and heroine possession, armed robbery, selling gun permits, concealing stolen property, and hiring a contract killer.

It is probably fair to say that for every substantiated instance of police misconduct there are likely to be five to ten more that either were not reported or were not satisfactorily substantiated. The police are notorious for protecting one another and, notwithstanding the dedicated efforts of police internal affairs departments, investigating police corruption still is about as effective as goats guarding cabbages. The 1972 Knapp Commission Report found evidence of payoffs to plainclothes police officers from gambling interests in New York City to range from $400 to $1,500 monthly for each officer. In 1993, another investigation found the practices discovered by the Knapp Commission to be alive and well. Gambling payoffs, however, are small potatoes when compared to narcotics-related payoffs, which run into the hundreds of thousands of dollars.

Citizens can't afford to monitor police and other enforcement officials because of bureaucratic secrecy and the size and complexity of the law enforcement process. Simply learning enough about the ins and outs of law enforcement to be able to identify a corrupt official is a daunting task even for a trained lawyer. Prosecuting attorneys and police officials have wide discretion over whether to press or drop investigations, and most of the decisions they make are not put on the public record. The Knapp Commission attributed police officers' reluctance to investigate or prosecute other officers to "intense group loyalty."[21]

Although drugs represent only part of a much larger crime problem, drug addiction is our most serious crime-producing agent and a major cause of high property crime rates. In some metropolitan areas as many as 80 percent of all armed robbery arrests involve addicts. One study showed that, across five gradations of increasing narcotics use frequency (less than or equal to once per month, greater than once per month but less than daily, once daily, twice daily, and three or more times daily), approximate mean annual aggregate property crime rose from $200 to $1,000, $2,700, $9,500, and $13,000, respectively.[22]

21. See B. L. Benson, "An Institutional Explanation for Corruption of Criminal Justice Officials," *Cato Journal* (Spring-Summer 1988).
22. See G. Speckart and M. D. Anglin, "Narcotics and Crime: An Analysis of Existing Evidence for a Causal Relationship," *Behavioral Sciences and the Law* 3 (Autumn 1985).

Studies of correlations between property crime rates and the fluc-
tuating street value of heroin have revealed a conclusive positive relationship. When the price of the drug increases, the incidence of
property crime correspondingly rises. In contrast, violent crime that
does not involve financial gain is not correlated with street heroin
prices. During the East Coast heroin shortage of 1972, drops in se-
rum hepatitis rates, an indicator of heroin use prevalence, were accompanied by regional decreases in property crime. Likewise, concerted efforts to stem the flow of heroin into the Washington, D.C.,
area and attract addicts into treatment markedly decreased property
crime in the area.

All of this comports with common sense. When a person spends
large amounts of money for heroin or crack, does not deal drugs, and
has no source of legitimate income, crime is necessary to support his
or her addiction. Although most addicts have had histories of arrests
before their addictions, the coexistence of addict criminals and
criminal addicts does not alter the fact that heroin and crack addiction increase property crime levels dramatically. A high proportion
of addicts' pre-addiction crime consists of minor offenses, whereas
post-addiction crime consists of serious property offenses, often involving threats to the victim's person. One study of 243 addicts estimated that they alone committed half a million crimes in eleven
years.

More important, drug trafficking itself is making America a much
more violent country. In Los Angeles, adolescents as young as fifteen
roam the streets in Mercedes and BMWs, toting Uzi submachine guns
and Soviet-made AK-47 assault rifles. In 1986, more than five thousand
violent crimes in Los Angeles—including 328 murders—were directly
related to adolescent gang violence. The arrival of crack in the early
1980s created a billion-dollar underground economy in Los Angeles
that transformed both neighborhoods and the gangs that dominate
them.

Because of drugs, gangs are no longer groups of bored teenagers
engaging in petty crime; teenage gangs are now the distribution network of a state-of-the-art, billion-dollar industry. A typical Los Angeles
street gang may have two hundred members between thirteen and
twenty-six-years-old, and each gang will typically move between twenty-five and forty kilos of crack or cocaine a month. In Los Angeles
County, there are roughly six hundred such gangs, counting more than
seventy thousand active members. Although most gangs are either

black or Hispanic, there are Asian, Samoan, and white gangs as well. And now, as urban markets become saturated, small cities, suburbs, and rural towns are being invaded by big-city dealers, who are much more violent than the local criminals the police have been accustomed to handling.

In the small town of Martinsburg, West Virginia, about an hour and a half away from Washington by car, state and federal police arrested forty-six suspected dealers in 1986. All along the rural corridor that parallels Interstate 95 from Florida to New York, the Jamaicans have cornered the crack network. Small Town, U.S.A. offers easy profits to drug dealers at low initial risk because rural communities lack the drug awareness of big cities and are even less prepared than their urban counterparts to cope with naked savagery. Local police forces can be easily overpowered and even more easily corrupted.[23]

The unusual violence associated with all aspects of the drug business arises from a sinister combination of money, readily available high-technology weapons, and an utterly savage underclass willing to use both without scruple. The entire drug industry reflects the sociopathic recklessness of teenagers and young adults whose family-structure-related poverty and deprivation have immunized them to both hope and fear. They exhibit a casual acceptance of—and sometimes enthusiasm for—torture, murder, "drive-by" shootings, and public mayhem. This intense underclass savagery is partially the result of our successful integration programs. Urban ghettos no longer contain a middle-class of minority doctors, lawyers, teachers, merchants, and civil servants. The blacks, Hispanics, and members of other minorities who possess the money and skills necessary to do so have emigrated from the inner cities, isolating and concentrating the most desperate and least adaptable of all our people. Unlike the United States of yesteryear, however, upward mobility is not predominantly a one-way street; as the successful (like Wadud Ahmad) move out of the slums, teenage never-married mothers and divorced women with children move in.

Downward mobility engendered by illegitimacy, divorce, and parental neglect leads people into marginal activities of all sorts. Those who commit only so-called victimless crime like prostitution and drug dealing are, in fact, a much greater menace to a peaceful and well-or-

<hr />

23. See Malcolm McConnel, "Crack Invades the Countryside," *Readers' Digest* (Feb. 1989).

dered society than they would at first appear. Prostitutes and drug dealers bring with them into any neighborhood they chose to enter their customers—pimps, suppliers, and rivals—all of whom create real or apparent danger.

Studies such as the *Figgie Report on Fear of Crime* characterize the crime threat as "slowly paralyzing American society." According to the report, fear of violence directly affects four of ten Americans and indirectly affects roughly 70 percent of the population. Many polls, such as a Gallup poll conducted in March 1981, reveal that more than one-half of the public is afraid to walk at night in the area surrounding their home.[24] Whenever a neighborhood has a visible population of pimps, prostitutes, drug dealers, and the assorted derelicts whom these vice purveyors attract, the neighborhood appears dangerous and therefore becomes a frightening place in which to live.

Crime emerges from a breakdown of the traditional family and traditional neighborhood. Until we restore two-parent families and family neighborhoods across a broad front, crime will continue to increase. The persistent rise in the crime rate is the most atrocious form of public bankruptcy. In our attempts to combat crime with increased numbers of police, compensatory programs for neglected and soon-to-be delinquent children, prisons, prosecutors, and courts we only add more debits to a looming financial collapse. We are also bankrupting ourselves metaphorically in that in our efforts to be "nonjudgmental" and not to make anyone "feel bad" we are allowing the highest rate of downward mobility ever experienced in American history.

It is all well and good for media pundits and trendy social scientists left over from the 1960s to pontificate about how the two-parent, nuclear family is an institution of the past. Yet proposals for averting the social collapse that I have discussed in this chapter by techniques other than restoring the two-parent family through reducing illegitimacy and dramatically lowering the divorce rate amount to furnishing each family with a child-care provider paid on a civil service salary and benefits scale. That might work in some utopia, but it won't work in the world in which we all actually live. Until people recognize that fact, we in government can't do much for them.

24. National Opinion Research Center, *General Social Surveys—1972-1985* (Chicago, 1985).

6

Solutions

The hard part of a book like this is the last chapter, where the problems identified in earlier chapters must be solved. Although the picture is gloomy, I am optimistic that there are, indeed, solutions that are neither too expensive nor beyond our political capability. My basic premise in all of this is that the average American still has substantial civic virtue and is willing to act responsibly to make this country work. Illegitimacy and divorce do not emerge from deliberately irresponsible behavior; at the very bottom of the socioeconomic scale, a few fourteen-year-old girls may consciously decide to have children in order to escape brutal, oppressive conditions in their own homes. But this is not deliberately irresponsible behavior because fourteen-year-old girls don't know what adults know about the demands of parenting. Divorce is widespread simply because we have told ourselves over and over again that getting divorced when there are young children at home is *not* irresponsible.

When I present a summary of this book in speeches, the shock in some audiences tells me that what I have explained comes as a complete surprise. The great majority of adult Americans fail to understand how the transfer of family functions to government budgets is bankrupting governments and taking money from education, police protection, public health inspections, and infrastructure repair. And, as I indicated in the Introduction, the numbers involved in these transfers stagger the imagination. The total state budget for West Virginia Public Radio—an integral part of educational broadcasting—is about $700,000 a year.[1] Four premature babies who are conceived out of wedlock and must be in intensive care for the standard hundred days

---

1. Source: West Virginia Educational Broadcasting Authority, *State Appropriation for Fiscal Year 1992-93.*

at a cost of $2,000 a day will consume $100,000 more than the entire Public Radio budget.

Even in the face of examples like this, the urge to deny is nearly irrepressible. In audiences of extraordinarily bright high school seniors, such as participants in the West Virginia Youth Science Camp (which invites the two top science students from every state to West Virginia each summer for a three-week camp), many students view my lecture as an attack on their own upbringings in broken homes or as an attack on their mothers and fathers. Even more intense is the resistance of middle-aged persons, and that would appear to be related to feelings of personal guilt. Indeed, about half of all my audiences exhaust every alternative explanation for our public bankruptcy before finally acquiescing in the real explanation, if indeed they ever acquiesce at all.[2]

Guilt, however, is not the emotion that discussions of these matters should rightfully inspire. America has always extolled the value of change. Yet change almost invariably constitutes an experiment, and most experiments fail, whether they're conducted in physics, chemistry, or social relations. Americans who were either parents or children during the last thirty years were part of the greatest social experiment of all time, and many parts of the experiment actually worked. Our efforts to eliminate race discrimination and sex discrimination were part of this same experiment, and those efforts succeeded beyond the wildest dreams of anyone born before 1940.

I am essentially in the budget balancing, economic development, and crime fighting business and not in the morality, religion, and nostalgia business. Consequently, in the preceding five chapters I have been discussing family structures, not "family values." Society in general and state governments in particular are collapsing because of inappropriate family structures, not because of lack of "family values," at least as that

2. While writing this chapter, I spent four days lecturing at Dartmouth College. One of my hosts, a professor of philosophy in his late thirties, is married to a family counselor employed by a state-funded New Hampshire social service agency. Over lunch one day, my professor friend reacted to my assertion that we need immediate action to change private behavior in family-related matters by blaming the breakdown of families in general, and the plight of his wife's clients in particular, on the tightfisted policies of the Reagan-Bush administrations. No amount of explanation about how welfare-related budgets are even now voraciously eating money from everywhere else, or about how quickly any increase in taxes would be consumed by family-substitute programs, had the least effect in enlisting his support in changing private behavior. I had the feeling I was talking to a stone wall, and I attribute this intransigence from an otherwise brilliant, open-minded, and rigorously trained person to the strength of the denial reflex.

term is generally understood in today's political debates. Gays and lesbians are not part of America's bankruptcy problems because gays and lesbians do not produce children, do not transfer family costs to public budgets, and do not cause crime by adding to the burgeoning underclass. And, at the risk of losing my more conservative supporters, sexually active but responsible young people who meticulously use birth control and protect themselves from venereal diseases do not contribute to our bankruptcy because they neither bring poor children into the world nor otherwise strain public budgets.

Similarly, working mothers who arrange for high-quality day care are not part of our problem, and neither are hard-charging childless couples who both work fifteen-hour days. The same applies to divorcing couples whose children are grown. Gays, lesbians, sexually active youngsters, working women, and divorcing couples over fifty confound conservatives' notions of "family values," but none of these phenomena may be directly linked by hard empirical evidence to the collapse of government budgets, the deterioration of our labor force, or the rise in violent crime. That appropriate family structure—a two-parent family with many hours of direct parental or high-quality surrogate care-giving whenever children are present—is essential to a safe, educated, and prosperous society can, in contrast, be proven by hard empirical evidence.

Americans can become passionately committed to any program that looks like it might help society, which is why I maintain that simply talking about why we are going bankrupt in clear, no-nonsense terms brings us a considerable way out of our current dilemma. My favorite example of Americans' undertaking an enormous bother for absolutely no reward but the sense of helping their country is recycling. Recycling is a terrible annoyance. Furthermore, there is a limited and glutted market for recycled paper, bottles, and cans, so the recycling industry up until this point has not succeeded in becoming anything more than part of the garbage industry. Nonetheless, I recycle like a fiend, and so does every other state employee in West Virginia. My children demand that I recycle glass, cans, and newspapers at home, while environmentally sensitive secretaries and law clerks (who sometimes seem to have received Gestapo training) demand that I separate all my government trash and use the recycling bins that have been placed on every floor of state office buildings. In a country where a function as pedestrian as separating trash can be elevated by the middle class to almost a religious rite, it would seem that we could slightly reorganize family living arrangements.

That is why throughout this book I have again and again returned to the simple proposition that we must change the stories that we tell one another about family, work, and child care. Before we can begin to tinker at government programs that affect family structures, we must first agree on what family structures we want in the twenty-first century. Some divorces are necessary; some mature, economically prosperous women can raise happy and successful children alone; and many families successfully juggle two careers yet produce children who go on to win Nobel Prizes. However, as a general rule, illegitimacy, divorce, and double-income households where both spouses work like Trojans don't produce as good economic, educational, and social results as we get in two-parent households where one parent stays home to take care of the children, or, at least, both parents work hard in the nurture business and the father exerts himself to take up the slack created by a working mother (or the other way around).

In the early seventies, when I first ran for statewide office, I hired an experienced politician as my campaign manager. One day we were talking about the extent to which politicians need to give up their individuality to get elected. He pointed out that a serious candidate for a major office can grow a moustache, drive a sports car, use salty language, tell off-color stories in public, wear exotic clothes, and even take eccentric stands on public issues yet still get elected. However, he was quick to point out, although a candidate can do any one of these eccentric things, he or she absolutely cannot do two or three.

The same general rule concerning economy of eccentricities applies to a lot of the family-related matters that I have been discussing in this book. Murphy Brown, who is mature, rich, and smart, can successfully raise an illegitimate child because she can have full-time household help and has many educated, middle-class male friends to be father substitutes. Cynthia Johnson, who is fourteen years old, functionally illiterate, utterly destitute, and has no one to help her, cannot successfully raise an illegitimate child. Therefore, it seems to me that reforming family structures can proceed in a fairly nonjudgmental way. I have sufficient faith in the average American to believe that understanding the problem is the solution, which is why the fastest, cheapest, and most effective program for changing private behavior is the massive paid advertising campaign I shall outline in the second half of this chapter.

What I hope to have done in this book is to bring together empirical data from schools, work places, and the criminal justice system to show that in our national dialogue about "family structure" we are no longer talking about a menu of equally viable alternative "life styles," but rather about ironclad relationships between certain patterns of family life (or, really, lack of family life) and readily identifiable social pathologies. The empirical evidence is now so beyond cavil that the media, academia, and legislative committees have no choice but to rethink our attitudes about family matters.

Any new model for family life in the twenty-first century that relies on the transfer of family responsibilities to government budgets cannot work. The persistent budget deficits of California and New York, along with the precarious financial condition of most other states, should now conclusively put to rest any lingering hopes for workable social systems that do not depend on private parental investments in children. We can have good social insurance to protect us from life's unavoidable tragedies, but we cannot find enough premium money to finance a social insurance system that reimburses for tragedies of our own making.

My emphasis on changing stories is not thrown out in lieu of more specific and controversial proposals such as (1) completely abolish welfare; (2) completely restructure welfare; (3) fund high-quality day care for everyone who chooses to use it; or (4) provide a family allowance to stay-at-home mothers. Changing the stories we tell one another is rather a necessary precondition to any and all other tinkering. We need to know what system we will put in place of the system we have now. Once the stories have been changed, we can then begin to tinker at the thousands of little free-market and government incentives that affect our family behavior.

In designing policies that will help to solve the problems I have outlined, we must begin with the first rule of government policy: Whatever government subsidizes, we get more of, and whatever government taxes, we get less of. Ideally, we want more two-parent families where one parent either stays home or both parents work in such a way that stress is reduced (usually at the expense of income) and opportunities for nurture expand. We want fewer poor, single-parent families created by either illegitimacy or divorce. We also want fewer self-absorbed, overworked parents who ignore their children's emotional needs even while providing for them financially.

Ultimately, all decisions about tax rates, labor laws, social programs, health insurance, housing subsidies, and school curricula must be informed by our answer to the following question: Does this particular policy, in the long run, have the effect of strengthening or weakening the stable, two-parent family? Unfortunately, government can't stop doing what it is currently doing without pulling the rug out from under millions of people who relied on existing programs in setting up their lives. Radical reform that cancels existing support programs, therefore, has an extraordinarily limited political viability.

The existence of a welfare mechanism that allows young girls to set up their own households complete with a child (who, psychologists and gynecologists tell us, is often conceived in the expectation that it will behave like a live doll) encourages such households to be set up. Yet abolishing AFDC payments tomorrow will catch millions of people without any other means of support, which is why the likelihood of that happening is vanishingly small. Thus, notwithstanding all the palaver we have heard since the late eighties about "significant" reform in the welfare system, nothing—absolutely nothing—is going to happen in the real world of welfare reform. As Paul Offner, legislative assistant to Senator Daniel Patrick Moynihan, explains it:

> Only one significant reform has been approved since the federal welfare statute was first enacted in 1935: the Family Support Act of 1988. It passed with little opposition as the result of a historic compromise between liberals and conservatives: government must help welfare recipients obtain work skills, but recipients must reciprocate by attending classes. After that, they must work if they are able, preferably in the private sector, otherwise in a publicly funded job.
>
> That was the theory. In practice, the bill's drafters (of whom Clinton was one) knew Congress would not be able to fully fund the program. So they did the only thing they could: they dropped the requirement that all able-bodied recipients participate. Today only one in five eligible recipients is actually enrolled in the welfare reform program.[3]

3. Paul Offner, "Workfail," *The New Republic,* 28 Dec. 1992, 13.

In spite of the ire that welfare clients inspire in the average taxpayer, the obvious question is, Why haven't we done something about the "welfare culture" long before this? Part of the answer, of course, is that welfare (like social security) is a major vote-buying program, and tinkering at it is likely to lead to politician unemployment. But far more important is the fact that the vast majority of people on welfare are neither social misfits nor more lazy, unproductive, or unworthy than the rest of us. Rather, welfare clients are largely proud and caring, and they want to work in serious jobs. Most people who receive welfare are on the dole for only about three years, after which they get back on their feet.

West Virginia is almost an entirely white state. Our black population is roughly 6 percent, and we have very few minority residents other than African Americans. The Indians, Koreans, and Muslims in West Virginia are more likely to be doctors and engineers than they are to be shopkeepers or unskilled workers. In January 1993, the state's unemployment rate was slightly more than 10 percent—the highest in the United States—and it was estimated by William Carlton, professor of community medicine and an International Kellogg fellow at West Virginia University, that roughly 30 percent of all West Virginia families are eligible for some welfare program. Notably, West Virginia's high unemployment rate is primarily related to the automation of the coal industry (a process that has been going on since 1948)[4] and to the general decline of old, capital-intensive, rust belt industries like steel and glass manufacture.

Whenever just six or seven industrial jobs are advertised in West Virginia, there are lines hundreds—or even thousands—of people deep. What this demonstrates is that the reason we didn't tinker at the welfare system much between 1935 and 1988 except to make it bigger and more inclusive, and the reason that efforts at welfare reform in 1988 were halting and half-hearted, is that politicians—as opposed to the think-tank or university policy wonks—understand that, in all circumstances other than a boom economy, getting and keeping a job

---

4. In West Virginia, the coal industry employs a hundred thousand fewer workers today than it did in 1948 and forty thousand fewer than in 1976. In the three years immediately preceding the May 1993 contract negotiations between the United Mine Workers and the Bituminous Coal Operators Association, six thousand coal miners lost their jobs, bringing total coal employment to twenty-two thousand miners, of whom only 40 percent are now union members. See the *Charleston Gazette,* 9 May 1993.

that allows a person to feed a family is a lot easier said than done, particularly in the thousands of places that more or less look like inner-city Los Angeles or rural West Virginia.

What I have said here about welfare is hardly profound, but I mention welfare reform in this chapter on solutions simply to let the reader know that welfare reform is a dead end. The only change in the welfare system that might positively affect divorce and illegitimacy is to stop paying benefits, but there is little political support for such a drastic program, even from people like me. As a policy weapon, welfare reform is rather like poison gas in World War I—a weapon that can, on occasion, work but is more likely to be blown back in your face.

The current welfare subsidy for illegitimacy has, at best, a marginal effect on teenage behavior anyway. Young couples are not thinking about welfare policy as they begin their mating. Therefore, conservative "family values" advocates must recognize that we will make no dent in our current problems simply by cutting subsidies. If young people are going to continue to mate, and if welfare policy is the last thing that they're thinking about as they declothe, then there is no choice but to talk about improved birth control if we are interested in workable solutions. Our educational, economic, and social problems are now so severe that conservatives and liberals must reach out to one another to seek common ground. The extreme left wing and the extreme right wing may never be accommodated, but they at least are powerless in the face of compromises that satisfy the great middle.[5]

No subject except religion is as explosive as sex. Often advocates of "family values" have personal feelings about sex that make them maniacal on the subject of premarital intercourse and extraordinarily

5. This is why in Europe abortion is a political non-issue. Although abortion is totally outlawed in Southern Ireland and almost entirely unregulated in Sweden, the rest of Western Europe enjoys almost exactly the same legal structure about abortion. The compromise that has been achieved through the political process in such diverse places as Catholic Italy and Protestant Holland is roughly as follows: Women have reasonably free access to abortion, but there are certain hoops that must be jumped through in deference to reverence for life. Doctors must certify that an abortion is for the physical or mental health of the mother, and women seeking abortions must be informed of other available options. Furthermore, abortions must be done in full-service hospitals, not free-standing abortion clinics that advertise "in by ten, out by twelve." Although this compromise satisfies no one entirely, it is sufficiently acceptable to the political middle that neither the left-wing fringe nor the right-wing fringe can garner enough support to make a respectable noise. See Mary Ann Glendon, *Abortion and Divorce in Western Law* (Cambridge: Harvard University Press, 1987).

punitive toward those who believe in sexual freedom. Because, as those in the women's movement understand, children have the tendency to force women away from work outside the home, many fervent "family values" advocates have a thinly disguised agenda that goes beyond assuring children good nurture from someone—mother, father, grandparent, or high-quality surrogate—and would return all women to lives centering in home and hearth on the pretext that child raising demands it. At the same time, there are some activists on the left who maintain that teenage pregnancy is good for girls because it allows them to get their childbearing done early so that later they can focus on "serious work." Other activists on the left advocate more sexuality in general and would advance that agenda through "sex education" in the schools.[6] In short, it is easier said than done to get the left and right to work together, but all centrists, at least, have a certain reasonable streak, so with effort common ground can be found.

The compromise between the center left and the center right must contain a bilateral agreement. The center right must agree not to insist on sexual abstinence as the exclusive method for achieving birth control; the center left must agree to eschew "sex education" and other programs that would appear to encourage (or at least condone) out-of-marriage sexuality under the guise of teaching health and birth control. But the centerpiece of the great compromise must be that abortion is beyond the compromise's scope and will remain a free-standing issue not to be linked in any way to solutions to our public bankruptcy problems.

Within the center, then, proponents of a woman's right to choose must agree that none of the new resources specifically appropriated in response to the current crisis and as part of the plan for rolling back illegitimacy and curbing our excessive divorce rate will be used to promote abortion in any form. Abortion opponents, on the other hand, must agree that no new resources will be used to roll back existing legal rights to abortion. Of course, feelings run so high on both sides of the abortion issue that strident advocates will probably demand support for their positions as a type of "rent" for not torpedoing non-abortion-related programs. Obviously, that strategy will stymie all positive efforts to solve the public bankruptcy problem unless the center responds forcefully and unanimously.

Just as social liberals must be willing to emerge from denial and

---

6. See Dana Mack, "What the Sex Educators Teach," *Commentary* (Aug. 1993).

accept the fact that the two-parent family located close to grandparents and collateral kin still remains the best model for family life, social conservatives must forebear excessive nostalgia, accept the pervasiveness of sexuality in today's America, and willingly endorse preconception birth control, like Norplant, which does not rely upon discipline and foresight among youngsters who can muster little of either.

Carl Djerassi, the inventor of the contraceptive pill, and Étienne-Émile Baulieu, the inventor of the "morning after" pill, have both conceived new technologies to reduce illegitimacy (as well as other unwanted pregnancies), but in their autobiographies they express extreme bitterness toward the religious and political pressures blocking the introduction of better birth control techniques in the United States and around the world. In the United States, the process by which contraceptives are developed and introduced has become so expensive that most pharmaceutical firms have altogether abandoned manufacturing contraceptives just when we most need convenient and reliable technology.[7]

A cheap, safe pill that can be taken once a month and provides substantial tolerance for early and late dosage would improve contraception enormously among that part of our own population at highest risk. Many women, if they are uneducated, find it hard to take the current standard contraceptive pill regularly every day at the correct interval after each period. I sympathize with these women because I have the same problem. American men over thirty-five are usually encouraged to take about four aspirins a week, or half an aspirin a day, to reduce the risk of stroke. I attempt to take one aspirin a day except on Sunday, Tuesday, and Thursday because I have a hard time finding cheap aspirin tablets in half doses. Nonetheless, I end up regularly taking aspirin on the days I should miss and not taking aspirin on days I should take it. My doctor, a graduate of Princeton University and Columbia College of Physicians and Surgeons, springs for the more expensive and less easily found half doses because, he admits, trying to keep track of when to take a full dose is just too complicated. Consequently, it is hardly patronizing to point out that remembering when

7. I am indebted here and for what follows to M. E. Perutz's excellent review essay on *The Pill, Pygmy Chimps, and Degas' Horse: The Autobiography of Carl Djerassi* and *The 'Abortion Pill'* by Étienne-Émile Baulieu in the *New York Review of Books,* 8 Oct. 1992.

to take pills is not all that easy. There is, then, enormous room for improvement in our birth control technology, particularly when we are talking about fourteen-year-old girls.

Ironically, although the religious right (for want of a better term and implying no disrespect) have successfully cowered politicians into total avoidance of the birth control issue in our legislative bodies, it has really been the courts, through the expanding law of product liability, that have unintentionally done the most to discourage research and development in contraception in the United States.

The product liability system that works reasonably well to protect people from defective cars and exploding soda bottles does not handle well the peculiar problems related to drugs or vaccines. Genetic diversity ensures that there will always be some people in whom even the safest drug produces adverse effects. If the percentage of such people is substantial, then the adverse effects show up in clinical trials carried out on several hundred people before the drug is released on the market. But if the adverse effects manifest themselves in, say, only one person out of ten thousand, then the probability of the adverse effects showing up in clinical trials is negligible. When, however, any new drug is later used by millions, and affected persons sue the manufacturers for negligence, litigation expenses and damages may cost the firm producing a new drug millions of dollars. It is this exposure that makes research in an area like birth control uneconomical.

One would think that this problem is so obvious that it could be easily solved. But such is not the case because the structure of American state courts, where product liability law is created, virtually guarantees irrational results in product liability. America has fifty-two uncoordinated state or statelike jurisdictions, each of which is entitled to generate wildly eccentric product liability law. A responsible policy toward birth control drugs on the part of one court may not be followed by any of the other courts. If I rule that in West Virginia a person who suffers adverse side effects from a birth control drug is entitled only to net economic losses—that is, uninsured medical expenses, lost income, and special life-support equipment—I have no assurance that judges in other states won't drive up the price of birth control drugs by adopting a far more generous rule for their own constituents that may include big damages for pain and suffering as well as punitive damages.

If all the other state supreme courts don't buy into my responsible program to, say, encourage new and better birth control products, then all that I have done for my constituents is to divert product liability insurance money away from West Virginia to other less responsible states. Yet it is this very scramble for money from out-of-state manufacturers to help in-state plaintiffs that leads to a competitive race to the bottom and makes product liability law more and more of a hazard to manufacturers of medical products. This is why birth control research will not be undertaken to the extent necessary to develop breakthrough technology until Congress protects companies that do such research from bankrupting lawsuits through a "special case" statute that creates national product liability law for birth control products and will then be binding on the states.

Fear of liability not only retards development of increasingly effective birth control technology, but it also keeps some safe and useful products off the market. The $5.1 million verdict against Ortho Pharmaceutical Corporation for birth defects allegedly caused by its spermicide dramatizes this problem.[8] Subsequent to the verdict, experts who had testified that the birth defects were caused by Ortho spermicide repudiated their findings.[9] Even legal scholars who are extraordinarily enthusiastic about current product liability law when applied to ordinary manufactured products that are defective are critical of product liability law when applied to birth control products.[10] The *Ortho* court appropriately compensated plaintiffs for net economic losses; the problem was the open-ended damages awarded for future pain and suffering.

The one place where halting reform in product liability law has occurred at the national level (to eliminate the competitive race to the bottom) is in vaccine manufacture.[11] Vaccines are low-margin prod-

8. *Wells v. Ortho Pharmaceutical Corporation,* 615 F.Supp. 262, 295 (N.D. Georgia 1985), aff'd, 788 F.2d 741 (11th Cir. 1986), cert. denied, 479 U.S. 950 (1986).

9. Peter W. Huber, *Galileo's Revenge: Junk Science in the Courtroom* (New York: Basic Books, 1991).

10. See, for example, Jeff L. Lewin, "Calabresi's Revenge? Junk Science in the Work of Peter Huber," *Hofstra Law Review* 21 (1992): 183, 202, 203.

11. H.R. 5186, signed into law by Ronald Reagan on November 14, 1986, created a no-fault compensation fund under which payments will be made to the families of persons who suffer injuries or death as a result of receiving vaccines generally required by state law. Under the new scheme, persons seeking redress for vaccine-related injuries or death are required initially to file a petition for compensation through the no-fault fund in federal district court. A person establishing a vaccine-related injury or death may be awarded medical expenses, death benefits, lost earnings, and attorneys' fees.

ucts because they are administered once or only a few time in a recip-
ient's lifetime. They therefore generate only slight profits but possible
huge losses due to product liability litigation expenses and damage
awards, so the sale of vaccines usually represents an unacceptable risk
to manufacturers. In fact, a public health crisis occurred when many
manufacturers withdrew from the vaccine business and those manufacturers remaining were able to raise prices to such an extent that
price alone discouraged immunization in low-income families wherever public authorities were not aggressive in providing free immunization.[12] The problem became so acute that in January 1993—virtually
as his first important official act—President Bill Clinton asked for more
than $300 million for a national vaccine program and stated publicly
that he intended to seek price concessions from vaccine manufacturers.

The difference between vaccines and contraceptives is that there
is no political lobby against vaccines the way there is against contraception. However, the same product liability problem that exists in
vaccines exists in contraception. Currently, the cost of birth control
pills in the United States is higher than in any other advanced country
because of a product liability insurance premium included in the
price of every package and because of the excess profits made by
American manufacturers due to the limited number of producers.[13]
Consequently, we need a national statute, binding on the states, that

---

Awards for pain and suffering are limited to $250,000, and punitive damages are not
allowed. In the case of death, a lump sum of $250,000 is awarded.

However, the homogenizing effect of this legislation is vitiated by sections of the law
permiting a plaintiff who is unhappy with an award under the fund to reject the award
and sue the manufacturer in state or federal court. These sections do establish some
uniform standards concerning the manufacturer's liability, but they place no limits on
the kind or amount of compensatory and punitive damages that may be awarded.

12. In the 1950s, polio afflicted fifty-seven thousand Americans, whereas only four
cases were reported in 1984. No less dramatic was the decline of whooping cough,
brought about by the pertussis component of the DPT vaccine. The incidence of pertussis in the United States dropped from more than 265,000 cases and 7,500 deaths in
1934 to fewer than two thousand cases and only four deaths in 1982. Yet, as the incidence of preventable diseases declined, the incentive to be vaccinated against such diseases also declined, particularly among the poor and uneducated.

13. In most places, all conventional methods of birth control are subsidized by public authorities and private charities (Planned Parenthood, for example). Although this
helps a great deal, county or city health departments are still not like discount drug
stores with branches everywhere; access to subsidized birth control is often inconve-
nient, unpleasant, and even demeaning.

limits product liability exposure for birth control manufacturers but then assures quick settlements for net economic losses for injured victims. Here is a middle ground where moderate pro-choice and moderate right-to-life advocates should agree, and where we should all work together. I suspect that even the Catholic church would not actively oppose such an undertaking in light of the widespread use of birth control among committed practicing Catholics.

The greatest advance in birth control since the birth control pill is Norplant—a matchstick-sized contraceptive that is surgically inserted into a woman's arm and prevents conception for roughly five years. If a thirteen-year-old girl is given Norplant, she is safe from conception until she is over eighteen. If every girl in America at age thirteen got Norplant, most of our troubles with an expanding underclass would be over. We wouldn't necessarily abolish poverty or eliminate the underclass entirely, but we would stabilize its size so that antipoverty programs would have a chance to work.

I dwell on female contraceptive devices because they are far more reliable than are male contraceptives. Condoms, although useful in preventing AIDS, nonetheless require foresight, discipline, and a sacrifice in pleasure. Given what we know about men, condoms are not sufficiently user-friendly to make them "reliable." Surgical procedures like vasectomies are expensive, painful, and involve substantial risks that in some cases they may be irreversible. If, however, birth control research is encouraged and a pill or surgical implant for men is developed, everything that I say here about encouraging Norplant will apply with equal strength to the male alternative.

Unfortunately, Norplant is most vociferously supported by the wrong people, including the infamous neofascist State Representative David Duke of Louisiana as well as entirely respectable, but conservative, pro-life Republicans like State Representative Kerry Patrick of Kansas and Governor Pete Wilson of California. Both Representative Duke and Representative Patrick introduced legislation that would pay poor women to have Norplant installed, while Governor Wilson added an extra $5 million to his Office of Family Planning in 1993 to make Norplant more readily available to poor women. In short, what has happened in the Norplant debate is that the message is correct but the messengers are unattractive. Perhaps I am a more attractive messenger because I come from a state that is almost entirely white. Furthermore, West Virginia was among the first states to ratify the Equal

Rights Amendment (for which I voted as a legislator), and almost all of our current statewide officeholders have publicly supported freedom of choice.

In targeting for a Norplant experiment the county in West Virginia with the highest illegitimacy rate (31.9 percent), I would choose McDowell County, which also has the highest black population (13.5 percent) among our fifty-five counties. However, if I were then going to target the county with the second highest illegitimacy rate (29.7 percent), I would choose Clay County, which has our lowest per capita black population (0.1 percent). In West Virginia, the areas with the highest overall rates of illegitimacy are not cities like Charleston, Huntington, and Wheeling that have large black populations, but rather our Scots-Irish rural areas like Clay County, where everyone looks as if he or she could have stepped directly off the *Mayflower*. In West Virginia, some counties that are 8 percent black have lower illegitimacy rates than counties like Clay with almost no black residents (Figure 4).

The ideal solution to our illegitimacy problem is to offer girls between thirteen and twenty free Norplant (which, unfortunately, now costs $350 for the device, $90 for insertion and $84 for removal) along with sufficient financial incentives to go to a clinic and have the procedure.[14] In West Virginia, a $200 cash payment would be sufficient to attract as many women in our high-risk groups as could be attracted by any reasonable amount of money, and the same probably applies even in high-cost-of-living areas. To be politically acceptable, however, the program must apply to everyone within a specific geographical area. Obviously, poor women will be more inclined to participate than upper-middle-class women, but even if a Rockefeller or a Vanderbilt wants to participate, she should be welcomed if she lives within the geographical area. After Norplant is installed, women participating in the program should be paid $50 for undergoing a yearly checkup to assure that the device is working properly. Older women meeting income eligibility criteria might also be entitled to free Norplant and free check-ups, and selected high-risk groups like the developmentally disabled should be allowed to remain in the cash incentive program indefinitely.

14. Any program such as the one I am suggesting here would bring down the cost of Norplant significantly. States are now negotiating volume discounts on Norplant the same way that they negotiate discounts on office machinery and everything else that they buy in bulk.

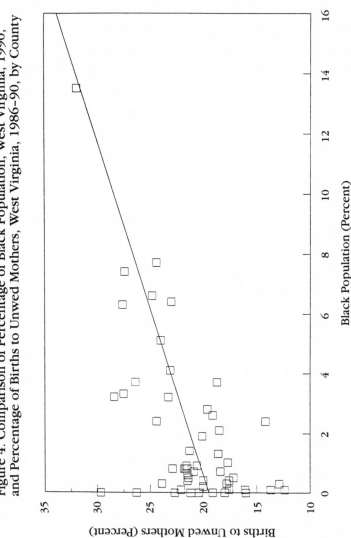

Figure 4. Comparison of Percentage of Black Population, West Virginia, 1990, and Percentage of Births to Unwed Mothers, West Virginia, 1986–90, by County

Black Population (Percent)

Births to Unwed Mothers (Percent)

Note: Figure includes linear regression line.
Source: West Virginia Department of Health and Human Resources, Bureau of Public Health, Office of Epidemiology and Health Promotion, Health Statistics Center. Information from Gary L. Thompson.

Unfortunately, giving incentives for Norplant use is just one of hundreds of proposals that require a little money up front but will pay big dividends in the end. Educators, drug counselors, prison wardens, and every imaginable social service provider I know echoes the same refrain: The expenditure of a little up-front money on social services now is cheaper than (name one) ignorance, crime, drug pathologies, venereal disease, birth defects, or unemployment later on. In the real world, of course, investments seldom produce the expected returns (just ask anyone who ever bought a Houston apartment building or a West Virginia ski resort), and the lack of correlation between investment and return that is so visible in business is magnified in government because it is so easy in government to confuse means with ends. Indeed, in government we can continue to spend the up-front money in response to provider pressure without ever seeing the promised return (or much giving a damn that we don't). Consequently, arguing for Norplant incentives—which in addition to being politically controversial can cost some real money—is like spitting against the wind.

A practical proposal is to provide Norplant with financial incentives to residents of certain high-risk areas. Once it can be proven empirically that Norplant with incentives will more than pay for itself in reduced medicaid costs alone in eighteen months (two gestation periods)—which is what I believe to be the case—then the program can be expanded to larger and larger geographical areas with smaller and smaller high-risk populations. Inevitably there will be accusations of "racism" because in the urban states—if not in places like West Virginia, Vermont, and Kentucky—the highest-risk groups in the highest-risk areas are disproportionately black. Therefore, regardless of any statistical rank orderings among different areas and different income groups, it is absolutely essential that some of the first areas targeted in every state look more or less like Clay Country, West Virginia, where everyone is white.

I realize that all of this leaves me open to charges of racism and elitism, but what is the practical alternative? By "practical alternative" I mean an alternative that does not spend unreasonable amounts of money and does not presume a technology that has not yet been developed. In devising real solutions, we must keep in mind that we always get more of what we subsidize and less of what we tax; we can use either the carrot or the stick. In other poorer societies, girls who get pregnant and the boys who make them that way end up getting the stick, often in the most literal sense. For a host of reasons, from anxiety over a "double standard" to concerns about possible racism, we are unwilling to adopt the cheap but efficient Islamic expedient of giving every unmarried sexually active girl a good flogging. And, of course, we can't tax illegitimate mothers because they don't have any money. So what's left?

And now, finally, we come to the centerpiece of this whole book and to the proposal that is both politically and fiscally feasible—a massive advertising campaign to explain what is happening to us. This proposal is, perhaps, a bit shocking at first because the United States is much more reluctant than developing countries to use the television and radio for the delivery of public health messages bought and paid for by the government. Yet, private organizations (and occasionally some government agencies) provide public service announcements that stations are asked to run for free. What I propose is that the government sell public health the way Proctor and Gamble sells soap or Coca-Cola sells soda pop. When we are talking about divisive political matters (like whether to raise taxes or invade Cuba) propagandizing with paid media is entirely inappropriate.[15] However, in publicizing public health dangers we should not be hesitant to use advertising paid for by the government along with all our other media tools. In discussions of polio immunization, for example, there is no First Amendment requirement to provide a "balanced discussion" by soliciting the opinions of advocates for the endangered polio virus.

Although the state and federal governments seldom resort to paid commercials, the media currently present health information in a

15. This is not the place to discuss constitutional law, but perhaps a little explanation of the constitutional limits on propaganda is in order. At heart, constitutional law is about refereeing the political process to guarantee that all decisions and all political coalitions are ultimately reversible. When we say, for example, that America is governed by a "rule of law" rather than a "rule of men," we do not mean that men (and women) aren't powerful in the most personal and mean-spirited possible sense during their tenures in office. Indeed, anyone who has ever relied for his or her living upon government contracts understands just how powerful a mayor, governor, or even U.S. senator can be, and anyone who has ever practiced law understands the old rule that "good lawyers know the law; *great* lawyers know the judge!" Nonetheless, we are still governed by a rule of law in the sense that there are regular occasions when we can turn the rascals out. Thus, what much of constitutional law is really about is protecting us from what has become typical in third world countries: one man, one vote, one time. The purpose of the First Amendment, then, is to guarantee that the party in power does not acquire a monopoly of the vehicles of communication, and to this end we must be circumspect about the extent to which we permit government to use the media to propagandize.

straightforward, responsible way that carefully evaluates conflicting scientific opinion and uses limited time to give good bottom-line advice. When there is genuine dispute among experts, the media attempt to report both sides, but the media never argue against such things as vaccination or exercise, nor do they argue in favor of such things as smoking and indulging in high-fat diets. Indeed, to the extent that illegal drug use is dropping outside the underclass, the reduction in drug use is probably attributable to a one-sided media campaign undertaken by private charities and the broadcast companies that included the famous television commercial showing the frying egg with the voice-over saying, "This is your brain on drugs!"

Between 1977 and 1984 I worked closely with the West Virginia Department of Human Services and frequently appeared in public service television commercials produced by DHS. By then we knew the economic effect of divorce on women and children, so the purpose of my commercials was to explain the consequences of divorce for all parties involved, but particularly for children. In the commercials, I stressed the trauma to children of losing the companionship of a parent and the significant reduction in income for all family members when a divorce split a household and eliminated the economies of joint living. The local television stations liked the commercials, which we issued three at a time about every six months, and so the stations ran those commercials for free as public service announcements.

Although I do not have hard data, anecdotal evidence from relatives of couples thinking about divorce, from lawyers, and from the staff at DHS indicates that these television commercials (which were aired at best only a few times a week for perhaps a quarter of the year) prevented as many as a thousand divorces over three years. That's not exactly spectacular in a state with almost two million people, but then again, the spots were run only to fill time that no one had bought—usually late at night or during the afternoon—and our production was primitive, relying as it did on dry text presented by one talking head.

As indicated in chapter 2, probably as many as 20 percent of divorces are unavoidable. Even in 1950, when America had far fewer crime and school problems than we have today, more than 20 percent of all couples divorced. However, we did not have the 50 percent divorce rate that we have today. Obviously, if we could reduce the divorce rate to something around 25 percent, both dollar demands on the social welfare system and the social costs "externalized" by family breakdown would be reduced significantly. None of this is impossible, or even unreasonable, because most experienced observers of my acquaintance—judges, lawyers, psychologists, social workers, child advocates, and domestic counselors—agree that as many as half of all divorcing couples will be made substantially worse off (in a long-term sense) by their divorce. The object, then, is not to enslave people who really need a divorce by keeping them in miserable marriages, but simply to explain in detail the ramifications of divorce to people who have not spent years studying this subject and who must be given credit for wanting to do the right thing.[16]

In Los Angeles the domestic courts have begun mandatory mediation in divorce cases to weed out those marriages (particularly marriages with children) that are unnecessarily being dissolved and to facilitate amicable child custody arrangements. The mediation program has not caught on outside Los Angeles, however, because the mediators and supporting staffs are expensive professionals. Furthermore, most lawyers don't like mediation because mediation makes litigating a divorce more time-consuming for lawyers and, therefore, more expensive for litigants already strapped financially.

Custom-crafted mediation, then, is not cost-effective for solving the social problems that divorce creates, although it may be of substantial value to specific divorcing couples. Although there exists a provider constituency composed of psychologists, counselors, and social workers who would like to put court-annexed mediation on the front burner, mediation is far too expensive to be useful in cutting the divorce rate in half. Our divorce problem is a public health problem; consequently, the programs that will work probably look a lot more like public health measures than they do the expensive individual procedures performed by private clinicians. The old public health doctor with his frayed collar, rumpled tweed suit, and beat-up Model T Ford, it should be remembered, prevented far more disease through regular restaurant inspections, elimination of open sewers, and universal vaccination than the fanciest clinicians at places like Massachusetts General Hospital ever cured.

Let us therefore focus on broad-based, public health-type approaches to divorce rather than individual, clinical approaches. Divorcing

16. I refer those who would like detailed support for my assertions here to my book *The Divorce Decision: The Legal and Human Consequences of Ending a Marriage* (New York: McGraw Hill, 1984).

couples must understand the following: (1) divorce makes both husband (if he pays his support obligations) and wife much poorer because it destroys the economies of joint living; (2) after divorce, fathers usually lose touch with their children because in most divorces
mothers get custody, and although visitation rights and joint custody
may keep fathers in touch, in the final analysis, remarriages, reloca-
tions, and continued bickering usually mean that fathers become more
and more removed; (3) mothers seldom if ever receive the entire
amount of alimony and child support ordered by the court, and in a
high percentage of cases mothers receive nothing for long periods or
nothing ever; (4) unless the marriage is so bad that wife and children
are physically abused or severely abused psychologically, studies show
that the children will be much worse off, and that the children will
have a much higher statistical likelihood of becoming delinquent, failing in school, or resorting to drugs if they come from a broken home;
and (5) new spouses often resent their partner's children from an earlier marriage and always resent alimony and child support payments
to a former spouse.

   In West Virginia, our court system is currently considering a requirement that all litigants in divorce cases watch a video program
about these matters. By the time one or both partners have hired lawyers, paid fees, and prepared themselves emotionally for a divorce,
however, the best opportunities to save their marriage have probably
gone by. We must then act preventively; we must buy time on every
television station at prime time and all other hours to provide people
with accurate public health information about the emotional, financial, and the externalized costs of divorce before they settle on such
an action.

   Although I believe that these paid advertisements should employ
all the techniques of Madison Avenue, I also believe that the content
must be straightforward health information. Fortunately, there has
been so much study of family-related pathologies during the past
thirty years that the things people most need to know emerge from
study after study where findings have been replicated. Thus, one
advertisement need do no more than make the following well-docu-
mented point: "Children in divorced families are nearly twice as likely as those in intact families to drop out of high school. Among all
children who drop out, those from divorced families are less likely
eventually to earn a diploma or a GED." However, I do not suggest a

"talking head" commercial by a public health doctor in a white coat. Professional ad producers must figure out how to make the proposition I've just stated memorable through background scenes, music, cartoons, and diagrams.

Numerous other simple messages that emerge from neutral studies will quickly change the way people think about family matters. We do not need to tell people how to live their lives; it is sufficient if we explain the consequences of certain courses of action. Here, then, are three more examples of commercial content, although again I would expect entertaining and engaging professional production:[17]

Half of single mothers in the United States live below the poverty line, although only one in ten married couples lives below the poverty line. Many other single mothers live on the edge of poverty. Even single mothers who are far from poor are likely to experience persistent economic insecurity, and divorce *almost always* brings a decline in the standard of living for a mother and her children.

Divorce causes children to lose contact with their fathers. In divorced families, only one child in six saw his or her father as often as once a week in the past year. Almost half of all children from divorced families did not see their fathers at all in the past year. Ten years after a marriage breaks up, more than two-thirds of children report not having seen their fathers for a year.

Nationally, more than 70 percent of all juveniles in state reform institutions come from fatherless homes. Boys from single-mother homes are significantly more likely than other boys to commit crimes and to wind up in the juvenile justice, court, and penitentiary systems. The relationship between growing up with a single parent and crime is so strong that controlling for family configuration erases the relationship between race and crime and between low income and crime.

A $100,000-a-day advertising budget on average in each of our ma-

17. I am indebted here, and for the previous example, to Barbara Dafoe Whitehead's excellent article "Dan Quayle Was Right," *The Atlantic* (April 1993). She reviewed the scholarly literature to uncover those findings that had been consistently replicated about family structure.

jor media center cities would cut our divorce rate in half and reduce our illegitimacy rate by more than half. The total cost of such a concerted effort is about $2 billion a year. Cities like Los Angeles and New York, of course, would get substantially more than $100,000 a day, and cities like Charleston, West Virginia, and Boise, Idaho, would get substantially less. After the first few years, yearly budgets would be much smaller because the divorce and illegitimacy prevention program could be kept alive the same way that Coca-Cola keeps its name recognition alive—through heavy saturation for short periods.

The theme of poverty and bad parenting is common to both divorce and illegitimacy, so my sample commercial on the relationship between growing up with a single parent and crime might emerge in two incarnations. The first would relate the statistic to divorce, and the second would relate the statistic to illegitimacy. In my estimation, the paid commercials aimed at illegitimacy will probably pay even bigger dividends than those aimed at divorce. No mother, regardless of social class, wants her son to spend half his life in prison.

One thing that elected officials do more than anyone else who isn't a teacher is spend time with school children of all races and all classes. I have been visiting decidedly ordinary working-class schools for more than twenty years (although I have never worked with big city children), and I am constantly amazed at how earnest and civic-minded these children are; indeed, the child who is shoplifting today is likely to be part of a school project to feed the homeless tomorrow. Some children, of course, are just plain rotten, but the great majority are like the rest of us—they would like to be nobler, more responsible, and more self-sacrificing than they in fact are. But then everyone's reach must exceed his or her grasp, and in this regard our children are like ourselves. Children, in fact, far more than adults, are looking for a cause. Therefore, once the anti-illegitimacy campaign hits a certain "critical mass," I expect the children themselves to take over and create positive peer pressure that will extend very deeply into even the fringes of the underclass.

Although $2 billion is a lot of money, using the media for public health messages has already been proven cost-effective elsewhere in the world where private decisions to have large families are stifling economic growth. As Dan Cogan, a reporter for the *New York Observer*, explains it:

Believe it or not, there's good news about trash culture. In fact, the soap opera, television's most degenerate medium, may just save the world. At a time when critics whine about American culture sinking into a televised wasteland, family planning and population control advocates are using soaps to curb population growth in the developing world. Broadcast during prime time on television and radio, the programs try to convince audiences to use contraceptives and even to desire fewer children.

The two major nonprofit groups sponsoring projects, Population Communications International (PCI) and Population Communications Services (PCS), trumpet their manipulative designs. "Towards the Use of Commercial Television," a widely circulated pamphlet by the Institute for Communications Research, a Mexican-based media research group, is replete with statements like: "We think it is of fundamental importance to understand the intellectual, emotive, and instinctive areas [of the brain], and the processes inherent to each one, to be able to appeal to them through television stimulation, and thereby achieve the change of both individual and social worldview." Roger Pereira, producer of a PCI-sponsored soap opera running in India, boasts his show "will be manipulative, and it is what a lot of dictatorial regimes tried to do, but rather badly. We're doing it very subtly through entertainment."[18]

All of this sounds like *Brave New World,* but drastic problems demand drastic solutions. Population control in places like Egypt (where population rises by one million souls every nine months) has an urgency far more immediate than divorce and illegitimate children have in the United States. But simply because we are not already on the brink of starvation, civil war, and oppressive overcrowding,[19] is no reason to persevere in ignoring techniques that other societies

18. Dan Cogan, "All My Children," *The New Republic,* 19 Oct. 1992, 10.

19. I can remember that Shanghai was one of the most miserable places I have ever visited because there were always masses of people wherever one wanted to walk. At any hour of the day or evening, the shopping area called the "Nanking Road," which is only slightly smaller than Chicago's Loop, always had crowds equivalent to the crowds exiting Mountaineer Stadium at West Virginia University right after the West Virginia-Penn State football game. China will never be able to allow unrestricted private automobiles because there is not enough room for roads, even if the country had the money to build them.

have found successful in solving critical, population-related public health problems.

Notwithstanding the desirability of the $2-billion-a-year advertising budget, one enormous obstacle stands in its way: The public health advertising program is not promoted by a powerful provider lobby. Once we begin to talk seriously about a public information campaign, however, large provider lobbies will emerge, but their scheme will be to send teams of workers into the community to preach birth control and to do divorce "counseling." Many grants for the birth control part of this scheme have already been given. (I remember reviewing one in 1971 when I was chair of the Marion County Board of Public Health.) But sending out teams to persuade consumers is not the method that Cheer detergent or Coca-Cola selects to reach scores of millions. Obviously, if sending out teams were cost-effective, Coke and Cheer would be using that system.

Finally, I must confront perhaps the most explosive of all family structure issues—the double-income couple that has no time for their own or anyone else's children. What makes this issue explosive is that encouraging "stay-at-home" parents is not gender-neutral. In blue-collar families and heartland America, the parent who usually stays home (unless the man has lost his job or works at home) is the mother because women who work full time earn only about 65 percent of what men who work full time earn.[20] The fact that women *should* be paid as much as men does not change the fact that they are not. Furthermore, nearly all studies have shown that when given a choice, many more women than men will voluntarily choose to stay home and raise their children.

In 1977, at what in hindsight was perhaps the apogee of militant feminism, Sharon Araji of Washington State University conducted a study that asked what respondents believed the proper division of family labor should be and then asked how, in fact, such work was divided in the subject's own household.[21] More than two-thirds of those asked how child care should be divided responded that the division should be equal. When asked about actual performance, howev-

20. As of March 1991, the average woman who worked full time earned $22,768, whereas the average man who worked full time earned $34,886. Table 713, *Statistical Abstract of the United States* (1992).

21. Sharon Araji, "Husbands' and Wives' Attitude-Behavior Congruence on Family Roles," *Journal of Marriage and the Family* 39 (May 1977): 309.

er, those same subjects overwhelmingly responded that it was the woman who bore the brunt of child-care duties. Thus, sharing responsibility for child care would seem to be more a cosmopolitan pretension than a common practice.

A University of Nevada study that same year found that division of labor within the household was resistant to change.[22] Moreover, responsibility for the maintenance of children was among the duties least often shared. To the extent that husbands participated in child care at all, they were more likely to be involved in playing, baby-sitting, and disciplining rather than in such mundane practicalities as feeding, changing, and bathing. The Nevada study is significant because it examined cohabiting couples as well as married ones. One might think that those cohabiting would exhibit more "progressive" attitudes toward division of domestic responsibilities, but the study found that such couples exhibited a remarkable adherence to the sexual stereotypes of the world in which they grew up.

Finally, a study of professional couples undertaken at San Diego State University found that even among highly career-oriented women it was taken as a given by both spouses that the women had the primary child-care responsibilities.[23] The role of mother was seen as far more limiting than that of wife. One of the study's crucial findings was that the decision to take primary responsibility for children was frequently a voluntary one for women who saw parenting as a fundamental part of a successful female life.

Usually the women who write for the *Washington Post*, edit books, produce television programs, or hold tenured professorships enjoy their jobs and make enough money to buy high-quality, individualized day care. But happy and rich female executives are about as rare as their male counterparts. Scores of women work outside the home only because they must work in order to make ends meet. (Indeed, these women are no different from the scores of millions of men counting the days to their retirements.) My classy executive secretary, who makes $34,000 a year and who typed this manuscript, would be out of the law business tomorrow if she or her husband won the lottery.

22. Rebecca Stafford, Elaine Bachman, and Pamela Dibona, "The Division of Labor among Cohabiting and Married Couples," *Journal of Marriage and the Family* 39 (Feb. 1977): 43.

23. Norma Heckman, Rebecca Bryson, and Jeff Bryson, "Problems of Professional Couples," *Journal of Marriage and the Family* 39 (May 1977): 323.

Furthermore, if the woman lawyer who works as my permanent law clerk had her druthers, she would be staying home with her five-year-old son.

Consequently, when we discuss solutions to the problem of unsupervised neighborhoods, the lack of stay-at-home parents to watch children, and the lack of volunteers for schools, scouts, and other neighborhood activities, it is important not to confuse the women who currently work eight-hour shifts at 106 degrees Fahrenheit down at the local headlight manufacturing plant with Hillary Clinton, Sharon Rockefeller, or Zoë Baird. There are plenty of parents around who desperately want to stay home but are prevented from doing so by either financial need or social pressure. Furthermore, the problem of social pressure is probably even more prominent with regard to men who would like to stay home or, at least, cut back their working hours because the culture of the locker-room discourages men from emphasizing their nurturing roles. We can't do much about the financial need for either women or men, but we can do something about social pressure and locker-room culture.

In 1991, the accounting firm of Price Waterhouse did an analysis for the *New York Times* on the value of a second earner in a typical midwestern blue-collar family.[24] The accountants' figures demonstrated that in suburban Minneapolis, for a married couple with one child under age four where the husband earned $25,000 a year and the wife earned $16,000 a year, the net value of the wife's second income was $6,036 a year, or 29.8 percent of total family income. In addition to federal, state, and local taxes, the wife's net earnings were reduced by $3,129 a year for day care, $780 for work clothing, $702 for commuting, and $1,040 for lunches and coffee.

Ironically, the same study found that for a professional couple in New York City, when the husband earned $70,000 a year and the wife earned $50,000, the net value of the wife's second income was only $5,909, or 12.3 percent of the total combined family income. In this example, city, state, and federal income taxes took $36,785 from the joint income, social security tax took $7,749, and child care took $15,600. Work clothes, commuting, and lunches were about twice what they would have been for a blue-collar worker in Minneapolis.

24. Tamar Lewin, "For Some Two-Paycheck Families, the Economics Don't Add Up," *New York Times*, 21 April 1991, E18.

The unfortunate thing about these numbers is that in blue-collar families the contribution of the working wife is large enough that the work force participation rate of women with children at home cannot be reduced significantly without some type of wage replacement. That, in turn, would cost big money in two regards. First, paying twenty million couples $2,000 a year for one parent to stay home would cost $40 billion a year. In addition, the parents who stayed home would not be paying income and social security taxes, which would cost, perhaps, another $80 billion.[25] Furthermore, a big part of the subsidy would go to parents who are already staying home, and the subsidy would still not be big enough—even at $2,000 a year—to replace even half of the net income lost by the second worker in most double-income families.

I point all this out simply to show that it is fruitless to linger over facile solutions like "family allowances" that even a rough estimate will disclose to be idiotic so long as the United States has a $3 trillion national debt that is rising by more than $300 billion every year. Although European countries—particularly France—do subsidize families and have a host of interlocking programs designed to increase family size and provide reasonable child care, the most important parts of these programs could not be easily transplanted here.[26] Cash allowances for children in France begin only with the third child. Therefore, the primary subsidy for families emerges from the steeply progressive French tax structure. For a married couple there is a two-person deduction; for a family of three, there is a two-and-a-half-person deduction; for a family of four, there is a three-person deduction; and there is a full one-person additional deduction for every child, beginning with the third child. For us to adopt anything that looks like the French system would require that we restore the pro-family progressivity that we had in our tax code in the sixties—something that is politically impossible given the number of unmarried and childless voters.

25. These numbers are very rough and do not emerge from a sophisticated model. They are inserted here simply to provide an estimate of the order of magnitude of the cost of an income replacement program. Obviously, the order of magnitude is something between $100 and $200 billion; it is not between $10 and $20 billion.

26. In France, a pregnant woman receives an award of 8,000 francs (roughly $1,454) conditioned upon her seeking prenatal medical care and following the doctor's advice. That we could do. French employers are required to give an unpaid two-year maternity leave, and that we could also do.

In France, children may enter a government school at the age of two. However, French schooling tends to break down into five weeks of school and two weeks of vacation all year long, except for the slightly longer summer break from about July 8 to September 8. Consequently, French parents have the same problem caring for their children during vacations that American parents have. What makes the French system work on balance better than the American system is the much lower level of geographical mobility in France. Roughly one-half of all Frenchmen live within twelve miles of their parents, so child care is regularly performed by grandparents and other relatives. There are, of course, professional child-minders who take children before and after school, and there are excellent camps for the vacations through which children can go off with young counselors to ski, bicycle, ride horses, or just play around near home at a much more reasonable cost than programs of comparable quality in the United States.[27]

Europe in general, and France in particular, has something to teach us, but the lessons relate more to the value of adult children living close to their own parents and the continued viability of extended families than to tax policies or family allowances. In this regard, one conclusion that appears fairly inescapable from a study of crime and related matters in the United States is that both stay-at-home parents and stay-at-home grandparents benefit entire neighborhoods as well as their own children and grandchildren. Consequently, staying at home is something that we want to encourage, which means subsidizing it whenever the occasion arises. The disparities in average wages between men who work full time and women who work full time forces me, from considerations of honesty, to admit that when we talk of "one parent staying home" we are, on average, talking about the mother. However, notwithstanding averages, increasingly there are instances when the woman earns substantially more than the man and the

---

27. I notice this most prominently during the winter at European ski resorts. An American is well advised to schedule his or her own vacation around weeks when big cities like Paris do not have the winter break, which is staggered among different regions through February and March exactly so that the ski resorts like Chamonix and Courcheval can avoid being overcrowded at any one time. Children come by the thousands to places like Chamonix and Courcheval, led by college-aged counselors, and the whole group stays in barracklike accommodations with communal meals and good deals on lift tickets and ski equipment rentals. From my observation over the years riding on the lifts with these children, the campers are polite, well behaved, and appear to be cheerful and happy about their ten days in the mountains.

woman is even more committed to an outside career. Nothing, of course, would serve to lower the crime rate more than adult men staying home and asserting leadership in the community, and, indeed, many men are now beginning to do this, or they are at least coming to share the child care and housekeeping duties. This is a hopeful sign, but to date it is largely a middle-class rather than a working-class phenomenon.

The need for income makes it difficult for most families to afford a full-time parent, but things like flexible working hours, six-hour days, and more part-time work with opportunities to buy such full-time benefits as group health insurance would go a long way toward helping families fill the nurture gap without unreasonably lowering their living standards. In my own office, we employ all of these techniques. Fortunately, we produce a product—namely written court opinions and court orders—so when during the week those products are turned out is immaterial. I am the only person in my office who deals with customers directly, and that is when we hold open court, so my hours in some regards are the least flexible of all. Some operations, like my chambers, lend themselves to parent-friendly working arrangements; others, of course, like AT&T long-line repair or coal mining, don't. But the fact that some operations can't be made more flexible is no reason not to tinker at other operations that with a little imagination can be made more flexible.

Although it is not possible to initiate a $120-billion-plus wage replacement program, over the next twenty years we can realign incentives through the tax code, family leave policies, and mandatory "mommy track" options. "Mommy track" options (or, quite possibly, "daddy track" options) will allow stay-at-home parents to advance to senior positions in government, the professions, and private industry at a more leisurely pace than the current "up-or-out" system that forces all ambitious people to work long hours during the years when adults usually have young children at home.[28]

28. The term *up or out* originated in the U.S. military, where commissioned and noncommissioned officers are given a certain number of years to be promoted from one rank to the next. After twenty years of active-duty service, a person in the military may retire with a pension equal to about half his or her base pay plus medical care and the privilege of using military facilities. However, if a person fails to get promoted from, say, captain to major in the five or six years allotted, he or she will be required to leave the commissioned ranks of the service before retirement. This same pattern is now also seen in law firms, where young lawyers are given a certain number of years, usually

Fortunately, some significant reduction in the parental labor force participation rate can be achieved immediately and almost for free. Many women work more for self-esteem and prestige than for the extra money, and if more self-esteem and prestige were to attach to being a full-time mother and homemaker, the female labor force participation rate would drop noticeably if not precipitously. Almost every adult well enough educated to read this book has been in a social setting where a deafening silence, a patronizing comment, or an apologetic smile followed a woman's confession that she was "just a housewife." Men who would like to be full-time parents have an even harder row to hoe in this regard.

In the free market, stay-at-home parents aren't paid money, whereas parents who work outside the home are. Much of the second-earner parent's income, however, is illusory; it is only the externalization of child-related costs that allows outside work to appear profitable. Most jobs—taxi driver, waitress, factory worker, coal miner, government office worker—don't carry prestige beyond that associated with "employed" rather than "dependent" or "unemployed," but all these jobs do engender self-respect. If we change the stories that we tell one another to reflect actual costs and benefits in terms of the educational, economic, and social contribution of stay-at-home parents, greater self-respect will attach to parenting, and we will get more of it. This message must be included in our $2 billion-a-year advertising budget because it fits in nicely with the whole "nurture" theme.

In proposing these solutions, I believe that I have stayed within the realm of the politically possible. Indeed, my last proposition—that we can noticeably change the percentage of both mothers and fathers who stay home simply by giving full-time parenting more prestige—depends on the success of this book and others like it in crystallizing our thinking about family-related pathologies and how their costs are externalized.

My other proposals are cost-effective and well within the realm of

---

about six, to make partner. If a young lawyer is not invited into the partnership within the allotted time, he or she then must hit the bricks and find a new job. Today women rightfully object to the twelve-hours-a-day, six-days-a-week rite of passage to become partners because these long hours deprive them of any opportunity to spend time with their children. Men also object, but they are less vocal about it because placing family life ahead of career goals is not yet considered an appropriate attitude among the leaders of the locker-room set.

fiscal possibility. The advertising budget of $2 billion a year for anti-illegitimacy, antidivorce advertising will be recaptured immediately on lower medicaid payments. The paid advertising program should be placed in the capable hands of the Office of the Surgeon General. The enabling legislation should absolutely forbid the creation of a government staff greater than five persons to administer the paid advertising part of the program. The thing America does better than any nation on earth is entertainment and advertising, and a campaign of this type is best contracted to experts outside the government who have already made fortunes promoting Cheer and Coca-Cola. Thus, I want guys and gals working on this project who look like Walt Disney and the grey-flannel-suit crowd at Benton and Bowls; I don't want to rely on folks who look like the clerks at my local post office, the media super novas at my local PBS station, or the imaginative bureaucrats who run the Washington, D.C., Department of Welfare.

Part of the reason for demanding real professionalism in the paid advertising program is that a lot of people already live in single-parent homes as the result of either divorce or illegitimacy. Although there is no choice but to convey the strong public health messages that I have suggested throughout this book, there is no reason that we shouldn't insist on surpassing tact so that we don't shatter the feelings or undermine the self-esteem of those for whom the die has already been cast. I don't know how to do this, but I am sure it can be done by the geniuses at Walt Disney Studios. I doubt that it can be done by the standard, uninspired civil servant.

If, in the initial Norplant program, we target one million high-risk females (at least half of whom should be white) at an average of $500 apiece, including the cost of the device and the administration of the program, then we are talking about another half a billion dollars. If, within eighteen months (or two normal gestation periods), it becomes obvious that all the cost of this program is returned in saved medicaid dollars, then the program should be expanded and refined.

I have suggested the subsidized use of Norplant because I believe that technically such a program would work and be cost-effective, but I know that politically the Norplant proposal is much more difficult to implement than even the public health advertising campaign. In terms of a practical strategy, the advertising campaign comes first and is the lynch-pin of the whole endeavor. After two years of $2 billion a year in advertising, the illegitimacy rate will not only have dropped by roughly 50 percent, but everyone's consciousness will also have been raised about how illegitimacy leads to overall educational, economic, and social collapse. It is at that point, then, when political resistance will be much lower than it is today that the Norplant program can be used for "mopping up" the highest-risk populations whose behavior has been most resistant to modification through public health information. Then, the Norplant program itself will have a further consciousness raising effect and lead to broader Norplant use among women for whom it is provided at government expense but who are not actually paid to use it.

After more than twenty years in government, working on problems largely related to family structure, I have surpassing faith that the two programs that I have suggested will work beyond our wildest dreams. Of course, it is an axiom of democratic politics that controversial programs don't get funded. Although $2 billion for one or two years and another $500 million for the Norplant experiment as soon as it becomes politically possible is small beer compared to the cost of a fighter wing and just about equals the $4.515 billion we have given to El Salvador since 1981,[29] it is, nonetheless, a lot of money that could be used for traditional pork projects that would put tens of thousands of low-skill people to work.

If congressmen and senators believe that the Catholic church, the National Organization for Women, the National Association for the Advancement of Colored People, the 700 Club, the faculties and students of "politically correct" universities, and other assorted left-wing, center and right-wing groups will all oppose some part of the program as I've outlined it, Congress will opt for defense or road repair pork. Therefore, the big solution is for everyone, including clerics, feminists, right-to-lifers, university faculty, and civil rights activists to think carefully about the propositions I have laid out in this book. The big lobby for a coordinated federal program should be state governors and big city mayors who are currently on the receiving end of the budget crises I have described and who can't print money or raise taxes.

If those who would oppose a family-structure advertising campaign and Norplant can think of something else that is feasible and does not

---

29. See Murray Kempton, "Truth and El Salvador," *New York Review of Books,* 23 April 1993.

rely either on technology that hasn't yet been invented or billions of dollars (like the money to provide income replacement for married parents with children) that can't possibly be found, then that's wonderful. But if there is no workable alternative program to the one I have laid out here, it is everyone's obligation to get behind the solutions I have outlined, because if we don't, America is going to get poorer and more dangerous still.

Index

RICHARD NEELY is a justice of the West Virginia Supreme Court of Appeals, where he has served three terms as chief justice. A graduate of Dartmouth College and Yale Law School, Neely served as an army artillery captain in Vietnam, practiced law by himself in the small mountain town of Fairmont, West Virginia, and served one term in the West Virginia Legislature. Since his election to his state's highest court in 1972, he has written seven books, served as William Frederick Atherton Lecturer at Harvard University, published regularly in national magazines including *The Atlantic* and *The New Republic,* and has spoken widely before lay audiences on government, law, and economics.